TRISTAN BERNAYS

Tristan Bernays is a writer and performer from London. His work has been performed at Soho Theatre, Bush Theatre, National Theatre Studio, Roundhouse and Southwark Playhouse.

His show *Teddy* won Best New Musical at the 2016 Off West End Awards, and he was a member of Bush Theatre's Emerging Writers' Group 2016/17.

Credits include *Testament* (VAULT Festival; dir: Lucy Jane Atkinson); *Frankenstein* (Watermill Theatre/Wilton's Musical Hall; dir: Eleanor Rhode); *Teddy* (Southwark Playhouse; dir: Eleanor Rhode); *The Bread & The Beer* (Soho Theatre/UK tour; dir: Sophie Larsmon); *Coffin* (King's Head Theatre; dir: Oliver Rose).

www.tristanbernays.com / @tristanbernays

Tristan Bernays

BOUDICA

NICK HERN BOOKS
London
www.nickhernbooks.co.uk

A Nick Hern Book

Boudica first published in Great Britain as a paperback original in 2017 by Nick Hern Books Limited, The Glasshouse, 49a Goldhawk Road, London W12 8QP

Boudica copyright © 2017 Tristan Bernays

Tristan Bernays has asserted his right to be identified as the author of this work

Cover photograph by Nick Arthur Daniel

Designed and typeset by Nick Hern Books, London
Printed in the UK by Mimeo Ltd, Huntingdon, Cambridgeshire PE29 6XX

A CIP catalogue record for this book is available from the British Library

ISBN 978 1 84842 686 3

Introduction

It's unusual to start a Monday morning at work watching
Gina McKee cut out someone's tongue – but that's what's been
happening in this morning's rehearsals, and I couldn't be
happier.

To be honest, I never dreamed I would be here in this rehearsal
room. Before *Boudica*, I wrote a play called *Teddy* – a play
unsurprisingly about Teddy boys in 1950s London. It was a
firecracker of a show – very loud and exciting, but in reality,
actually quite small. Just two actors playing all the characters.
My show before that, *The Bread & The Beer*, was a one-man
show about the ancient god of beer, sex and chaos, John
Barleycorn, being dug up in modern-day London – again with
just one performer (me, this time) playing all the parts.

So far, it had all been small plays. I was ready for something
big. Something huge. Something epic. A multi-narrative,
sweeping drama so large that no one would ever really produce
it. It would basically be a calling card to show I could 'write
big' so that, if any big theatres came a-knocking in some far-
flung, misty future, I could send it to them.

And that's where *Boudica* came in.

Many years ago, when I was still an actor, a close female friend
and actor told me she was sick of not having the fun that her
male counterparts got to have. Male actors get to have sword
fights, gun battles, car chases. Most parts for women, she said
(especially in Shakespeare and classical theatre), require them
to be beautiful and witty in a pretty dress, before they die
gracefully. Which is fucking boring.

Seven years later, when it came to writing this ridiculous epic
I had planned, I remembered this conversation and realised
I wanted to write something for women. Something where they

got to play complex and difficult characters – not just two-dimensional heroes or villains. More than that, I wanted to write a show for women where they got to have the fun. Where they got to wield swords and lead armies. Fight and destroy. Kill and be killed. Something where they got be warriors.

What better story than Boudica's?

Of course, no one would be foolish enough to produce a show which required around twenty characters, gods and queens and warriors and generals, sword and fist fights, buckets of blood and no less than three battles.

No one could be that foolish, surely?

Thank you to Emma Rice and Shakespeare's Globe for being that foolish. For wanting to put strong and complex female characters front and centre. For trusting me with their incredible stage. For letting me run riot and bring the story of this extraordinary woman hurtling into the twenty-first century.

Boudica may be two thousand years old, but we need characters like her. Now more than ever.

Tristan Bernays
London, August 2017

Boudica was first performed at Shakespeare's Globe, London, on 8 September 2017, with the following cast:

ENSEMBLE	Bethan Clark
CATUS DECIAMUS	Samuel Collings
ENSEMBLE	Owen Findlay
LUCIUS	Jenny Fitzpatrick
SILVIA	Kate Handford
ALONNA	Joan Iyiola
SEJANUS/SESTUS	Brian Martin
CUNOBELINE	Forbes Masson
BOUDICA	Gina McKee
ANDRASTE/ROMAN WOMAN	Anna-Maria Nabirye
BADVOC	Abraham Popoola
SUETONIUS	Clifford Samuel
BLODWYNN	Natalie Simpson
CLOTHEN/CATO	Tok Stephen

Director	Eleanor Rhode
Designer	Tom Piper
Composer	Jules Maxwell
Movement	Tom Jackson Greaves
Lighting Designer	Malcolm Rippeth
Sound Designer	David Gregory
Fight Directors	Rachel Bown-Williams and Ruth Cooper-Brown of RC-Annie Ltd

Acknowledgements

It takes an inordinately large number of people to get a play from page to stage, and I'd like to thank a few of them for their invaluable help, love and support:

Emma Rice – for programming us in the first place and letting us run riot in The Globe.

Matthew Dunster – for invaluable dramaturgical support.

Karishma Belani and Lottie Newth – for putting up with me during casting.

Jess Lusk – for being a woman who gets shit done.

Every staff member and volunteer at The Globe – for helping make this whole thing happen.

Eleanor Rhode – for continuing to work with me (despite all evidence suggesting she shouldn't) and for doing such a wonderful job bringing my words to life.

The cast, crew and creative team – for making the show so damn awesome.

Sarah Loader – for helping to get *Boudica* up and running at the very beginning.

Simon McBurney – we've not met but I definitely owe him a beer.

My agent, Katie Langridge – for endless feedback, help, advice and a whole heap of other stuff.

All the actors who helped in workshops and readings – without your time and effort, we wouldn't have got this far.

The London Library – there's nowhere better in the world to write.

Lucy – for love, support and reminding me to enjoy myself. You're good police, Champ.

Mum, Dad, Butts and Bakerloo – for not telling me to get a real job.

If I have forgotten anyone, please forgive me – I am a forgetful bugger.

T.B.
August 2017

This play is dedicated to women everywhere –
now more than ever.

12

Characters

BRITONS
BOUDICA, *Queen of the Iceni*
BLODWYNN, *Boudica's daughter*
ALONNA, *Boudica's daughter*
CUNOBELINE, *King of the Trinovantes*
CLOTHEN, *a Trinovantian lord*
BADVOC, *King of the Belgics*
ANDRASTE, *Goddess of Victory*
GUNNERVIK, *Tribal King*
WAYLEN, *Tribal King*
GUARD
DRUID
WARRIOR WOMAN
ICENIAN WARRIORS
BELGIC WARRIORS

ROMANS
GAIUS SUETONIUS, *a Roman General*
CATUS DECIAMUS, *Procurator of Britannia*
SEJANUS, *a Roman official*
SILVIA, *a captive Roman*
CATO, *Roman soldier*
LUCIUS, *Roman soldier*
SESTUS, *Roman soldier*
CENTURION 1
CENTURION 2
MESSENGER
ROMAN WOMAN

Time

61 AD

Place

Brittania, on the furthest western borders of the Roman Empire

Pronunciation Guide

Andraste – An-drass-tay
Alonna – A-low-na
Cunobeline – Kew-know-beh-lean
Gaius Suetonis – Guy-us Sue-toe-knee-us
Catus Deciamus – Kay-tus De-see-ar-mus
Prasutagus – Pras-yew-tay-jus
Camulodunum – Cam-yew-lod-yew-num
Verulanium – Ver-eh-lay-knee-um

*This text went to press before the end of rehearsals and so may
differ slightly from the play as performed.*

Prologue

Enter ANDRASTE, *Goddess of Victory.*

ANDRASTE.
When first they came, their ships did cut the sea
Like gleaming scythes; their shining armour burned
Our native eyes, and filled our hearts with dread.
They came from Rome, an empire which reached
From smoky tips of Indian East unto
The Afric' South of Egypt and toward
The cold Germanic North; and now its gaze
Was westward-fixed upon this little isle.
A seeming barren wasteland where they thought
No noble flower grew, but they knew not
That harsh environs breed a hardy weed
With thick strong roots – and so were the native clans.
A double dozen different warring tribes
Whose several kingdoms compassed this small isle.
The Celts and Picts, the monsters of the north;
The Belgics, fearsome soldiers, men of war
Whose blood and bravery was nonpareil;
The Trinovantes, skilled in word and trade,
Whose craft would make the god Hephaestus blush;
The Druids, shadow walkers, men of night,
Whose wisdom ran as deep as did the woods
Where gods like me and mine do darkly roam.
A hundred years, the Romans gave us siege;
A hundred times we tribes did drive them back
Through bloody battle and brave noble deed.
But we could not forever hold the tide
And soon the Romans claimed this isle as theirs
And we have since lain underneath their yoke
A broken, fractured isle of slaves and curs.
But many wore their slavish bonds with pride:

The client kings who made a pact with Rome,
Which in return for this did offer them
The Roman life of gilded luxury
And dazzled them with wine and song and wealth
Even as they robbed their kingdoms blind.
These client kings took Rome's gold offerings
And thought themselves as equal with great Rome –
But a chain of gold is still naught but a chain
And they were no more free than were their subjects
Who heavy felt the conquering heel of Rome
Grind their faces down into the dirt.
Now here we witness this: the funeral
Of one such client king, Prasutagus,
King of the Iceni (a noble eastern tribe:
Masters of horses, carriers of the spear).
His fellow client kings have come to mourn
And celebrate his life in liquor; while
Already Rome's imperial officer,
Catus Deciamus, has begun
To carve his lands and wealth up for great Rome.
But soon will come a figure to this scene:
The wife of Prasutagus, the Icenian Queen
Who comes to claim her kingdom – but perforce
Will come to claim the right of this whole isle
For those who live in it, and she will lead
These scattered, fractious tribes in unison
Against their tyrant masters. She will dip
Her javelin's tip into their blood and write
Her name in history so all will know
The warrior queen who made the Romans fear.

PART ONE: THE COMING STORM

ACT ONE

Scene One

The city of Camulodunum.

The feasting hall of Prasutagus.

Drums and noise – a funeral wake is in progress.

Enter several TRIBAL KINGS *alongside the Roman Procurator,* CATUS DECIAMUS.

They sing a drinking song for the dead – it's loud and raucous.

THE KINGS.
  When Death comes for me in my bed
  Let me be dressed from toe to head
  In gleaming armour, gold and ready
  To fight on the Other Side

  I shall not go me full of dread
  But glad of heart and full of bread
  My belly full of beer and ready
  To feast on the Other Side

  I leave me now the girl I've wed
  And take sweet Death unto my bed
  Buck naked, long and hard and ready
  To fuck on the Other Side

  *The funeral party continues to sing and celebrate as they
  exit, and the scene shifts to:*

Scene Two

Outside the feasting hall of Prasutagus.

Three ROMAN SOLDIERS *on watch –* CATO, LUCIUS *and* SESTUS.

CATO.
Sweet Pluto's arsehole – this fucking island!

LUCIUS.
What ails you now, Cato?

CATO.
What do you think?

SESTUS.
Mars, give me strength –

CATO.
This shitting, shitting cold. Clings to you like tar and rusts your joints. I shall die before the summer comes.

LUCIUS.
I don't think the summer ever comes here.

CATO.
This morning, when I awoke at the arsehole crack of dawn for our watch, I went to the latrine and I pissed icicles.

SESTUS.
Oh for the gods' –

CATO.
They cracked as they hit the ground, so hard it was – the soil had grown colder than a Teuton's ball sack. I had to chip one off the end of my cock with my dagger.

SESTUS.
You should have left it – you need the extra inches.

CATO.
For what? What flea-ridden savage would you have me fuck? Unless you have some Delphic beauty hidden up your tunic that you're willing to share with the rest of us.

LUCIUS.

He's got you there, Sestus. It's not just the cold that's making his cock shrivel. Have you seen the natives?

SESTUS.

I try not to look.

LUCIUS.

It'd put a man off his food, let alone fornication. I haven't got my end away in so long, my balls are as blue as berries.

CATO.

Oh, berries!

SESTUS.

Oh for fuck's sake – you've got him talking about fucking food again.

CATO.

I long for berries – for some real fruit.

SESTUS.

We'll be listening to this all fucking night.

CATO.

A ripe plum or figs dipped in honey.

LUCIUS.

It makes him happy.

CATO.

And lamb, slow cooked in rosemary.

SESTUS.

Well, it makes me fucking miserable! Listening to this mewling Umbrian bastard moan about the cold, the damp, the fucking food –

CATO.

What's wrong with Umbria?

SESTUS.

Since you left? Nothing.

Enter CENTURION 1.

CENTURION 1.
>Hail.

CATO, LUCIUS *and* SESTUS.
>Hail.

CENTURION 1.
>What news?

SESTUS.
>Besides Cato's whining, quiet as the grave, sir.

LUCIUS.
>How goes the feast?

CENTURION 1.
>As you would expect from savages.

LUCIUS.
>That bad?

CENTURION 1.
>The sight of their beer-soaked, hairy faces bellowing their
>island songs is enough to put any man off his food.

CATO.
>Is there any food left?

CENTURION 1.
>They toast the dead Icenian king as though he were a god
>amongst men.

LUCIUS.
>But didn't he desert them when they last rebelled?

CENTURION 1.
>What do you expect? Honour amongst barbarians? Pride
>goes out the window when they can fill their bellies.

LUCIUS.
>And now they drink to him as he lies dead.

CENTURION 1.
>Cold as this here earth.

CATO.
>Cold as a Teuton's ballsack.

SESTUS.

You ask me, the stupid monkey was wise to side with Rome when he did.

CENTURION 1.

Rumour is he was not so wise.

LUCIUS.

How so?

CENTURION 1.

The client king was not a frugal man. He careless cast off his newfound Roman wealth in wine, women and whatever else the savages care for.

CATO.

Doesn't sound too bad to me.

LUCIUS.

Has he no issue then? This client king?

CENTURION 1.

Rumour is there's two daughters and a wife – now Icenia's queen and on their way here.

SESTUS.

They are led by a woman? No wonder this backward island fell.

CATO.

Well, what should we do?

CENTURION 1.

What?

CATO.

If she comes here?

LUCIUS.

What do you mean, 'What should we do?'

CATO.

I've never met a queen.

SESTUS.

Queen? What fucking queen? There is no queen – just some filthy fucking ape in a fancy robe.

LUCIUS.

I'd like to see you say as much to her, Sestus. The girls
round here are liable to rip your balls off for less.

SESTUS.

I'd say as much to her hairy face.

LUCIUS.

Course, she'd have to find them first.

CENTURION 1.

Shut up and keep your eyes sharp for 'her majesty'. We've
already got one death being drunk to tonight – let's see if we
can avoid any more.

Exit CENTURION 1.

The SOLDIERS *resume guard.*

From elsewhere, enter BOUDICA *with her daughters*
BLODWYNN *and* ALONNA.

BOUDICA.

'Tis eighteen winters, daughters, since we have
Laid eyes again upon our feasting hall
At Camulodunum, our regal seat.

BLODWYNN.

It is more beautiful than I recall
Though I was scarce a babe since we did leave.

BOUDICA.

That day I can't forget – nor never shall.
Long have we been a stranger to that man,
Your father – once a king, now naught but bones.

ALONNA.

I saw you weep to hear the news.

BOUDICA.

                    I wept
Not for he, but this our home. I've dreamt
Of standing here again; but now I'm here,
I fear 'tis still a dream – that if I blink,
I'll wake and 'twill be gone.

BLODWYNN.

                    Then let us haste us
To this our hall. For too long we have lived
In self-imposed exile – I too have dreamt
Returning here triumphant; casting off
Our former life the fens and murky woods,
To lie in comfort –

ALONNA.

                  Sipping from a cup
Of purest gold.

BLODWYNN.

                  The walls brocade with drapes
And finest tapestries.

ALONNA.

                  Our fingers ringed
With silver and with jewels.

BLODWYNN.

                  Myself sat high
Upon my oaken throne in this my kingdom.

ALONNA.

                                    How
Do you say 'this your kingdom'?

BLODWYNN.

                          Sister – I
Am of the two of us the eldest, thus
It stands the throne is mine.

ALONNA.

                  And am I not
Our father's issue too? Am I not due
A portion of his kingdom?

BLODWYNN.

                    Worry not
For I your queen will see that you receive
Some – little land to call you 'home'.

ALONNA.

Blodwynn –

BOUDICA.

Enough!

You prate and prattle like two bickering girls.
Why did I take you from your father's house
Into the woods to teach you how to hunt;
To fight with bow and blade; to use the stars
As though your compass; to make from forest herbs
Restoratives and medicines; to talk
Unto the trees, the woodland gods themselves,
As kith and kin to aid you in your plight
For you to act so shallowly as this?
To be a queen is more than seeming grace
Begilded with a shallow glittering gold.

ALONNA.

We meant you no offence.

BOUDICA.

'Tis not offence
But foolishness you show – much like your father.

BLODWYNN.

You speak about him with such anger –

BOUDICA.

No,

Not anger, child – but disappointment. He
Was not always a shallow king – but when
The Romans came, he turned his back upon
His island and his people – and on me.
He argued joining Rome was the safer path.
I pleaded with him, cautioned him against
These oily Romans bastards; but he was blind
With Roman gold and silvered, flattering words.
He let himself be taken for a fool,
But I could never bear it. So I left
In self-imposed exile from the king.
But now it is our duty, daughters dear,

To raise our name again to those great heights
Where once Iceni stood in dreadful awe.
Let's inward to our feasting hall and thence
To take our rightful place upon its throne.

They approach the entrance to the feasting hall.

The three ROMAN SOLDIERS *are on duty.*

CATO.
Halt.

LUCIUS.
Who goes there?

SESTUS.
State your business.

BOUDICA.
What mean you 'business'? What 'business' do I need?
Why do you stand you guard outside my hall?

SESTUS.
Your hall?

LUCIUS.
Fat chance.

CATO.
This hall belongs to Pras– Prasu–

SESTUS.
Prasutagus.

CATO.
Him.

LUCIUS.
Did belong.

SESTUS.
Now it's property of Rome.

CATO.
So if you ain't got official business here –

SESTUS.

Move along.

BOUDICA.

Do you not know to whom you speak?

CATO.

Lady, we don't know who the fuck you are.

SESTUS.

So like we said before, if you ain't got official business here –

CATO.

Piss off and move along.

SESTUS.

Kitchen's round the back if you're after scraps.

BOUDICA.

I am no beggarwoman come for alms!

LUCIUS.

Wait.

SESTUS.

What?

LUCIUS.

It's her.

CATO.

Who?

LUCIUS.

Her – the dead king's wife.

CATO.

What? Her?

SESTUS.

Jesus, you're fucking joking me. Her?

LUCIUS.

Yeah.

CATO.

But – she don't even look like a queen!

BOUDICA.

I am the dead king's widow. I have me rights
To enter this his hall, to see his bones,
To speak me with the Procurator.

SESTUS.

Listen here –

BOUDICA.

I tell you I will speak to him, and if
You dare to keep me, then you'd best draw your sword.
Now – will you let me pass, or will you draw?

SOLDIERS.

...

The SOLDIERS *look at each other.*

SESTUS.

Alright. This way – your majesty.

Exeunt.

Scene Three

The feasting hall of Prasutagus.

The tribal kings CUNOBELINE, WAYLEN *and* GUNNERVIK
are singing and drinking with CATUS DECIAMUS.

CATUS.
   Kings of Britannia, noble friends of Rome,
   Drink we to Prasutagus, a valiant king
   And dearest friend, who was the very first
   To understand the guiding light of Rome
   Was never here to conquer, but to lead
   This island from the darkness to the light.

WAYLEN.
   We gladly drink to that, good Procurator,
   Especially with wine as good as this!

CATUS.
   My hearty thanks, my friend! It warms my soul
   To see so many of you here tonight
   Lay down your tribal enmities and come
   Tonight in peace as friends, and understand
   Prosperity and happiness awaits
   The friends of Rome.

GUNNERVIK.
                    Truer words were never spoke!

CATUS.
   Your courtesy does make me blush, my friends,
   Unless this wine has more to do withal!

WAYLEN.
   A toast to our host – Catus Deciamus!

They drink.

Enter GAIUS SUETONIUS – *a Roman General.*

GUNNERVIK.
   Good Procurator, I see you have a friend!

CATUS.
We do indeed – though his face looks too severe
To join our revels.

SUETONIUS.
Catus Deciamus?

CATUS.
The same. And who are you?

SUETONIUS.
Gaius Suetonius.

CATUS.
Gaius who?

SUETONIUS.
I wrote to you last month
With orders from the Emperor –

CATUS.
Oh yes!
Of course, I near forgot: the man from Rome.
You're early.

SUETONIUS.
Fair winds favoured my crossing.

CATUS.
Of course. Good friends, I bid you welcome this
Our new arrival, fresh from off the boat.
Gaius – Gaius –

SUETONIUS.
Gaius Suetonius.

CATUS.
Exactly. Bid you welcome him, my friends,
New general elect appointed to this isle
By he our most majestic Emperor
To oversee all matters military.

GUNNERVIK.
Welcome, general! Some wine?

SUETONIUS.

I'll not.

GUNNERVIK.
Why not? 'Tis finest Roman wine our host
Has brought to toast the life of our dead friend.

CUNOBELINE.
(*Aside*.) A friend that traitorous turned against his kin
And stood by Rome when first they did invade.

CATUS.
What say you, Lord Cunobeline?

CUNOBELINE.

I said

A wine so fine as this is a fitting drink
To toast so fine a friend as we have lost.

CATUS.
And those fine words to season this your toast.

GUNNERVIK.
Have you a drink, sir.

SUETONIUS.

No, I'll not

WAYLEN.

Come, come –

We are friends here – come share a drink with us.

SUETONIUS.
I will not drink. Come, are you deaf?

CATUS.
Forgive our general – he is but a soldier
And being such, he has a soldier's grace.
It's but a seeming brusqueness, honed from years
Upon the battlefield – pay him no mind.

SUETONIUS.
I would speak with you, Procurator, upon
Such military matters as needs must
Be soon attended.

CATUS.

Surely they can wait?

SUETONIUS.

I'm keen to start my tenure swiftly here
And would request your time to speak with me.

CATUS.

Very well – my friends, do go ahead
And take yourselves unto the feasting hall
To further now our revels. I will join
When Rome is answered. Till then, drink!

CUNOBELINE.

My lord,

I shall myself decline for I must go.
The road is long, the night draws in and I
Have business in my kingdom to attend.

CATUS.

How now, Cunobeline? You do not leave?
Our revels are but young.

CUNOBELINE.

And I am old.

CATUS.

Come come, you'll not desert our feasting hall
With such alacrity. If we were not
A surer man than this, we would now read
Your swift departure as a spurn to us.

CUNOBELINE.

Not so, my lord.

CATUS.

Come then, do not offend
My generous spirit leaving now so soon.
Stay but for one more drink.

CUNOBELINE.

My lord.

CATUS.

                           No – stay.

I do insist.

CUNOBELINE.

        Then, marry, I must stay.

CATUS.

Excellent. My friends, withdraw and dine.
This is our feasting hall, but here tonight
'Tis like a second home to you. Drink on!

The TRIBAL KINGS *leave.* CATUS *and* SEUTONIUS
remain.

CATUS.

Come then, Suetonius, since you insist
That we do interrupt our revels here
To talk of army matters, be you brief:
What need compels you leave Rome's warm embrace
To this sad frigid island?

SUETONIUS.

              In brief, the Druids.

CATUS.

Rome fears they will rebel again?

SUETONIUS.

                  Not fears,
But knows that left unchecked, it will be so.

CATUS.

And so you're sent to purge them from our isle
Before they can regroup?

SUETONIUS.

            If we're to keep
This land in Rome's imperial grasp, we must
Cut out this gangrene 'fore it rots the isle.

CATUS.

And does not Rome think I am capable
Of keeping them in check?

SUETONIUS.

                I do not know
What Rome does think – just know that I am sent
To clear these savages from off this isle.

CATUS.

Of course.
How goes it then? The beating heart of Rome?

SUETONIUS.

Full well, I should suppose. I am not wont
To keep abreast of gossip in the State.

CATUS.

No – I thought as much. I cannot see
A man as you – a soldier – bending knee
To fawn before great Nero's mighty throne
And whisper platitudes into his ear
In hope of table scraps or deferment.

SUETONIUS.

I serve the Emperor as does befit.

CATUS.

The Emperor? Strong words. Who would have thought
That after he The Madman, and then he
The St-St-Stutterer we would have got
A Pervert and a Mummy's Boy?

SUETONIUS.

                My lord –

CATUS.

Spare me your fawnings. This is not the Capitol.
This is the end of all the world, all but forgot
Except when Nero's purse is light of load,
And then we are beset with eyes from Rome
Who watchful hang and spy our every move.

SUETONIUS.

I come here as a soldier, nothing more.

CATUS.

Then as a soldier, let you be advised

That things are doing fine under my watch.
The savages respect me, hold me dear.
We have an understanding – if you will –

SUETONIUS.
I see your understanding with them.

CATUS.
                                        Pray,
Just what exactly do you mean by that?

SUETONIUS.
I mean me nothing, lord, save that you show
Your friendship drinking wine with savage apes.

CATUS.
Does it offend you? Seeing me break bread
With these my savages?

SUETONIUS.
                        Sir, I have known
Barbarians before.

CATUS.
                Yes, so I've heard:
The Terror of the Teutons, were you not?
The word is that all of Germania
Did tremble just to hear your name. Well then –
Let's see if you have earned that name; if you
Can make our Druids quiver in their boots.
You have permission. Head you north.

SUETONIUS.
                                    My thanks,
Good Procurator –

CATUS.
                Oh, thank me not.
I'm but a servant to his majesty,
No need for praise – my work's reward enough.

SUETONIUS *exits*.

A noise without – shouting and arguing.

The gods – cannot these savages sit still
For just a minute? Must they always fight
And bellow as though it were the end of days?

Exeunt.

Scene Four

The feasting hall of Prasutagus.

Enter CATUS DECIAMUS *to witness* BOUDICA,
BLODWYNN *and* ALONNA, *accompanied by the three*
SOLDIERS: CATO, LUCIUS *and* SESTUS.

CATUS.
What noise is this?

SESTUS.
My lord, we tried to make her wait while you were sent for –

LUCIUS.
– but she insisted.

CATO.
We told her that you were not to be disturbed.

CATUS.
And yet I am disturbed.

BOUDICA.

My noble lord.

CATUS.
Who speaks to me?

BOUDICA.
I am Boudica – the royal Icenian Queen,
And widow of dead King Prasutagus.

CATUS.
Guards, take your leave a while, and know we will
Make known if you are needed. Till then, disperse.

Exit SOLDIERS.

Forgive my men. You surely understand
That living as we do amongst your kind –
Many of whom hold little love for us –
Enthusiasm for... security.
My name is Catus Deciamus. I
Am Procurator of this outpost isle.
I knew your husband – though not yourself.
You're welcome, queen. And who be these two dams?

BOUDICA.

These are my daughters, sir, the rightful heirs
Of Prasutagus: Alonna and Blodwynn.

CATUS.

Well met to all of you and sympathies.
Your father was a – titan of a man.
Now pray what can I do for you? I beg
You haste for I have guests without,
Then soon must hence unto Londinium.
I cannot stand and prattle like some maid,
So, give me – briefly – the cause for this your suit.

BOUDICA.

Then know then, briefly, that my suit is thus:
No more than what is owed to me but half
Of Prasutagus' wealth and kingdom.

CATUS.

Half?

BOUDICA.

Aye, half, my lord.

CATUS.

And where came you to this?

BOUDICA.

Upon his death, the king had duly sworn
One half his wealth and kingdom over to Rome.
We do not argue this, but only come
For what is ours – the other half, which shall

As is the custom of Icenia
Be given to his daughters who shall rule
As queens when I am gone. This was his will,
Which had been sanctioned by the Emperor
In recognition of his duty borne
And of the debt that Rome to him did owe.

CATUS.
Speak you of debt? Then know that he, your king,
Was far from frugal in his royal ways,
And time and time again he courted Rome
For loans he did not pay. That money's owed
Unto the Emperor, and now with this his death,
We come to claim that which is rightful ours.
In short: his lands and title, treasures too,
And any other valuables we deem
As fit to pay the debt that he now owes.

BOUDICA.
But he had sworn me half.

CATUS.
Then he had sworn
A half that were not his.

BOUDICA.
I am his wife
And these his daughters – we are owed our due
By law.

CATUS.
Whose law?

BOUDICA.
Icenian law.

CATUS.
Such law
Has no authority within this realm.
This kingdom now is Rome, and being such
This land, this king, his will all fall beneath
The yoke of Roman law, which does decree

That never shall a female issue claim
The right of sovereign or inheritance
Which is the due of sons alone, fair queen.

BOUDICA.
This is not lawful.

CATUS.
Speak to me of 'law'?
Bid you remember, madam, 'fore we came
This island was a lawless wasteland, split
Midst warring tribes. 'Twas we that brought you law –

BOUDICA.
You lying bastard.

CATUS.
What say you?

BOUDICA.
You have
With usurious bonds and twisted words enchained
My husband to a lie and now will claim
My kingdom as your own and call it not
Plain thievery, but law.

CATUS.
Call you me thief?
I would advise you, woman, still your tongue.

BOUDICA.
What, Roman? Call me 'woman' to my face?
I am no churl, no scullion, farming wench,
I am a queen.

CATUS.
I see no 'queen' – only
A woman who has overstepped her bounds.

BOUDICA.
And I see nothing but a snake who knows
The law no better than the shit he spews.

CATUS.
> Again, I pray you mark her! Again with 'law'!
> The only law you brute beasts comprehend,
> Before we brought you ours, was fight or fuck.

BLODWYNN.
> What say you, Roman?

ALONNA.
> Know you not who she is?

BLODWYNN.
> Show you respect!

CATUS.
> And now her issue speaks!
> I bid you shut your stupid, stinking mouths
> Lest I be forced to shut them for you –

BOUDICA strikes CATUS.

BOUDICA.
> Do not speak to my daughters thus, you shit.

CATUS.
> How dare you strike –

BOUDICA.
> How dare you steal my lands,
> Take what is rightful mine, abuse my name
> And treat our royalty no better than dirt.
> This kingdom's mine, and I'll fight any man,
> A stinking bureaucrat or emperor
> Who stands between this land and me, I swear!

CATUS.
> I bid you guards, help me! Guards, help me – quick!

Enter SOLDIERS.

> This woman has abused me, and made threats
> Against the Emperor's life – arrest her, quick,
> And take m'lady to the central square,
> Then strip her of her vestments, bind her hands

Unto a wooden post, where she be flogged
Until her skin be split and broken, till
Her clucking tongue is stilled within her maw.
Take her.

The SOLDIERS *arrest* BOUDICA.

BLODWYNN *and* ALONNA *fight with the* SOLDIERS.

In the struggle, BLODWYNN *lashes out and strikes
a* SOLDIER.

They seize her and take her prisoner.

BLODWYNN.
    You fucking Roman bastard!

CATUS.

                            Shut your –

BLODWYNN *spits in* CATUS*'s face*.

Queen Boudica – since Roman law decrees
That daughters, when unwedded virgin things,
Are to their father property, we do
Lay claim upon your girls as rightful ours
And as a gift unto our hard worked men
Bestow these girls as playthings which they may
Take sport in as they please. Away with them.

BOUDICA.
    No! I beg you, Catus – please, I beg!
    You may do with me as you will: may break
    My bones in two, may tear my hair and flay
    The flesh from off my back, but do not let
    Your men abuse my girls –

CATUS.

                        They have wronged me.

BOUDICA.
    They are but children! Catus, I'll gladly take
    A triple punishment for them – but please, I beg
    Do not harm these my daughters. Catus. Please.

CATUS.

> You cries have stirred me so, madam, I could
> Almost be moved to show great leniency
> To these my prisoners – but they are mine no more.
> They are my men's. I gave them as a gift
> And once a gift is given, 'tis a flaw
> To beg the gift's return and break your word.
> I am a Roman, and a Roman without his word
> Is little more than nothing. Take them away.

Exit CATUS.

The ROMAN SOLDIERS *drag* BOUDICA *and her daughters offstage kicking and screaming,* BOUDICA *cursing his name and vowing vengeance.*

Exeunt.

Scene Five

The main square in Camulodunum.

BOUDICA *is dragged in by* SOLDIERS. *They rip the clothes from her back and tie her face first to a stake.*

They flog her until the blood runs to the floor and mixes with the mud and the dirt.

Meanwhile, BLODWYNN *and* ALONNA *are dragged screaming through the square by* SOLDIERS, *who take them away to rape them.*

ACT TWO

Scene One

A garrison in Camulodunum.

Enter SUETONIUS.

SUETONIUS.
    I'm eager to be far away and clear
    From Camulodunum, as well as he,
    Our worthy Procurator. I'd not trust
    The man with digging a latrine, though sure he'd fill
    One easily with what he speaks. That these
    The fingertips of our great Empire should
    Be trusted to a man like him. When I
    Was sent here, I was told I'd witness such
    Barbarian horrors: 'Wait, you're going where?
    The gods, you'll never make it out alive!
    I hear they eat their young and wear their skin!'
    But there's nothing here that I've not seen before,
    Just another bunch of savages –
    With different skin but savage all the same –
    Though truth be told they're no more dangerous
    Than the petty Roman bureaucrats who line
    Their pockets and their villas with stolen gold.
    I've often thought that I could throw all in
    With Catus and his kind, and grow me fat
    And wealthy, living off the sweat and blood of these
    Dull animals – why ever should I not?
    Have any of my years of soldiering
    Made any difference? Maybe. Maybe not.
    A hundred years we've been upon this isle,
    A hundred years – and nothing's really changed.
    The rich get rich; the poor stay poor; and me?
    I'm not employed to think. I'll leave all that

To Catus and his kind and head me north
To fight me with the rebel Druid hordes.

Exit SUETONIUS.

Scene Two

The main square in Camulodunum.

Before dawn.

BOUDICA *is bound to a stake in the ground. Her back is bare
and lashed with bloody marks.*

Enter SOLDIERS *with* BLODWYNN *and* ALONNA, *their
clothes torn, their bodies bruised and broken.*

SESTUS.
Begging permission for an audience with your most beloved,
royal and majestic highness!

CATO.
How's your back?

LUCIUS.
Did we scratch that itch for you?

SESTUS.
We bring you two girls –

LUCIUS.
Well, girls no more.

CATO.
Oh no – no, they are women now for sure.

SESTUS.
Oh yeah, we all agreed –

CATO.
The whole garrison.

SESTUS.

– that they did their womanly duties with great aplomb.
Now, take you, O mighty queen, these girls of yours and
high your royal arse out of the city and fuck off.

LUCIUS.

The Procurator in his great mercy has given you till dawn.

SESTUS.

And if he sees you or your little bitches ever again.

LUCIUS.

If he even hears from you.

CATO.

He will not be so lenient as he has shown himself to be.

SESTUS.

We take our leave and bid you goodnight, your highness.

CATO.

Most royal.

LUCIUS.

Most majestic.

SESTUS.

Long live the Queen.

Exit SOLDIERS.

ALONNA.

Blodwynn? Sister?

BLODWYNN.

Alonna?

They see each other – broken, battered and bloody.

BLODWYNN *tries to push herself up but she cries out in
pain, tries to hold back the tears.*

ALONNA *hobbles over to* BLODWYNN, *holds her and
comforts her.*

*Then they see their mother, half-dead and filthy with blood
tied to the stake.*

BLODWYNN.
Mother!

BOUDICA.
My daughters? Daughters dearest, is it you?
Come come, my little chicks, unbind my hands
That I may take you underneath my wings.

They untie BOUDICA *from the stake. She falls to the floor.*
They lift her.

Oh what is this? My daughters bear me up?
I do remember how I once bore you
Within my womb, and later in my arms
And dandled you as now you dandle me.
Your face, Blodwynn –

BLODWYNN.
　　　　　　　　　Please, don't –

BOUDICA.
　　　　　　　　　　　　Don't turn away,

My loves –

ALONNA.
　　　　　We can't – I –

BOUDICA.
　　　　　　　　　　Don't look so ashamed.
Do not these ruby mouths across my back
Cry likewise what I've suffered? And do you, dears,
Think any less of me for these my scars?
Though they have bruised and blemished you, you are
My daughters still, my blood, my dearest fruit
As dear to me as my own self.

BLODWYNN.
　　　　　　　　　　I am ashamed –

BOUDICA.
Speak not of shame, but flex your tongues like bows
That we may launch a thousand curses 'gainst
The bastards that have wronged us. Lift me up.

BLODWYNN.
No, Mother.

BOUDICA.

Up, I say.

ALONNA.

You are still weak.

BOUDICA.
Think you that I a queen will lowly sit
Upon the filthy ground and hang my head?

BLODYWNN.
Your wounds still bleed.

BOUDICA *stands*.

BOUDICA.

Then let them bleed. Let them
Full drain me of my blood till nought is left
And I am like a rock, my heart hard flint
From which will spring a vengeful spark so great
That all the Roman Empire may burn.
I swear by great Andraste, I shall not sleep
Till I have driven them from this our land.
I swear.
Now come, my darlings, come. We will away.
I hear the morning cock crow and the dawn
Will soon peep o'er the sky. We must make haste.

BLODWYNN.
Where shall we go?

BOUDICA.

We'll westward head and there
Seek sanctuary amongst the Trinovantes
And beg the king, the great Cunobeline,
To give us shelter while we plot revenge.

She lifts her daughters to their feet.

Exeunt.

Scene Three

Inside the feasting hall of CUNOBELINE.

Enter CUNOBELINE *and* CLOTHEN.

CLOTHEN.
How went the wake, my lord?

CUNOBELINE.
As you'd expect:
A dozen hearty kings all full of drink,
All belching songs, clapping each other's backs
Like dearest friends, when it was not yesterday
That they were face to face with brandished steel –
And all because the Procurator bids
We civil play in this his feasting hall.
'His feasting hall', mark you, Lord Clothen! As though
He did forget that hallowed hall belonged
To dead King Prasutagus, and not to he.

CLOTHEN.
'Tis not so much the king's now, but the queen's –
Wheresoe'er she be. The rumour is
She's east with her two daughters. Think you, lord,
That she'll return and claim what's hers?

CUNOBELINE.
Perhaps.
'Tis many years since she and I have spoke.
I know no longer how the lady thinks.
But till she comes to claim what's rightful hers,
'Tis still the dead king's hall.

CLOTHEN.
But for how long?

CUNOBELINE.
I know your thinking, Clothen. Stop you there.
I'm not inclined to wage me war with Rome
When we have seen the fate that did befall
Those kings that once resisted them.

CLOTHEN.

That fate

May come to all of us – no matter if
We 'civil play' with our invaders.

CUNOBELINE.

As long

As there's a chance of peace, I hold to it.

CLOTHEN.

And what when Rome tires of this here 'peace'?

CUNOBELINE.

I must as king safeguard my subjects' lives.
Rome is too strong. I would not risk the blood
Of these my people at such Roman hands.

Enter GUARD.

GUARD.

My lord, there's one at the gate who'd speak with you.

CUNOBELINE.

Who is he?

GUARD.

She, sir – a woman, if you please, though I would scarce
have thought her such. When first she crawled out the
darkness, we took her for some demon with staring eyes and
a voice like thunder –

CUNOBELINE.

Who is this woman?

GUARD.

She claims she is Queen Boudica, my lord.

CUNOBELINE.

Are you in earnest?

CLOTHEN.

It cannot be, my lord.

Enter BOUDICA, BLODWYNN *and* ALONNA – *all three
bloody, battered, bruised and soaked.*

CUNOBELINE.
By all the gods.

BOUDICA.
           My Lord Cunobeline.

CUNOBELINE.
What misery is this? Can it be you?
My friend and ally? And are not these two
The beauteous Blodwynn and Alonna? Oh,
What has become you?

BOUDICA.
           My friend, I will tell all –
But first I beg assist these daughters mine.
We have from Camulodunum walked night
And day in barefoot disarray, through fierce
And sulphurous storms, half-starved, half-dead, in need –

CUNOBELINE.
Say you no more – attendants! Look you to it.
Take these three 'dams to quarters, give them food
And water, bathe their wounds and give them rest.
With haste, I charge you!

BOUDICA.
           Take my daughters. I
Will stay with you, good king.

CUNOBELINE.
           You must take rest.

BOUDICA.
I'll take no rest, my lord, but we must speak –

CUNOBELINE.
But sure your wounds –

BOUDICA.
           I tell you I must speak!
Forgive my anger – 'tis not you, old friend.
I am exhausted, my nerves are torn and frayed.

CUNOBELINE.
Of course. Come – take the girls and care for them.

BLODWYNN.
  No, Mother!

BOUDICA.
                  Do not be afear'd, my loves,
  We're safe with friends –

BLODWYNN.
                              Don't leave us!

BOUDICA.
                                    Nay, come now –
  No tears, I charge you.

ALONNA.
                        Come sister, I'll bathe
  Your wounds and care for you. Come – let us go.

  Exit ALONNA *leading* BLODWYNN, *with* GUARD.

BOUDICA.
  'Tis many years since I stood in your hall.
  Who's this? Lord Clothen? Fie, you trenchant blade!
  Though many years unseen, you have not changed –
  But not so you, my Lord Cunobeline.
  There's something of a greyness in your locks
  And something of a girth around your waist.

CUNOBELINE.
  And you are just as flattering as ever.
  You always said I never would age well.

BOUDICA.
  And I was right. You look far worse than me.

CUNOBELINE.
  Time marches on, old friend.

BOUDICA.
                            Aye – that it does.

CUNOBELINE.
  We thought that we might ne'er see you again.
  Rumour had it that you had disappeared,
  Some thought you dead.

BOUDICA.

                    Do I look dead to you?

CUNOBELINE.
  We heard with woe the death of he, your king.
  I'm sorry for your loss. He was a great –

BOUDICA.
  I know, my friend, that you held he my husband
  In low regard.

CUNOBELINE.

              I never –

BOUDICA.

              Worry not.
  I do not blame you. The king had many faults
  Not least of which was cozening to Rome,
  Which has undone us quite – above all me.

CUNOBELINE.
  What do you mean?

BOUDICA.

                  They took my kingdom.

CUNOBELINE.

                                      Who?

BOUDICA.
  The Romans.

CLOTHEN.
          What?

BOUDICA.

                My husband's loyal friends
  Have robbed me of my land and title, and
  Have cast me down into this pitiful state.
  The Procurator scorned our pact with Rome
  And when I protested 'gainst this grievous wrong
  He had me flogged as though some common thief,
  Whilst these my girls were dragged into the fields
  By these his men who did defile them –

CLOTHEN.

By all the gods.

BOUDICA.

– but I'll not lay me down as I am told.
I needs must have revenge and so I ask
That you will join me – you and all your men –
That we will build an army and march south
And raze this Roman race to ruins; chase
This scourge from out our lands and then take back
This isle as rightful ours. Will you join me?

CUNOBELINE.

Boudica, my friend – what do you ask?

BOUDICA.

I ask for help.

CUNOBELINE.

You ask for suicide!
Do you forget the tyrant Caesar? Forget
How many lives we lost?

BOUDICA.

Have you forgot
How now these Romans rob you and your kin
Of all their land and wealth, and bleed you dry
Till soon you will be just as good as dead?

CUNOBELINE.

I have my people's lives to think upon
And must do what I can to keep them safe.

BOUDICA.

Even if that means whoring to Rome?

CUNOBELINE.

How can you stand there and insult me thus
When he your husband sold himself to Rome?

BOUDICA.

I am not my husband. I am no man
That quaking crawls on hands and knees before
The Procurator begging his favour.

CUNOBELINE.

You do forget yourself and loose your tongue.

BOUDICA.

I call things as they are, coward.

CUNOBELINE.

Coward?

BOUDICA.

Aye!

And a traitor too, that stands in my feasting hall
And drinks with he my enemy like dearest friends!

CUNOBELINE.

I swear by the gods –

CLOTHEN.

My lord and lady, peace!
What do you do? You two are friends of old –
Will you let Rome thus tear your love in two?
This is how we lose our isle – in hate
Of one another and not of they our foe:
The Roman whorsons living large and fat
On this our land, while we are left to scrounge
And fight amongst ourselves for table scraps.
If we are to defeat the bastards, we
Must stand united, not as enemies.
Then turn your ire not on those you love
But on the common enemy without.

BOUDICA.

Lord Clothen's right. Forgive me, noble king,
I spoke me out of turn. I should not thus
Abuse a cherished friend; but these my woes
Have made me hard against the ones I love.

CUNOBELINE.

Forgive me too, my friend – but can't you see
That it were madness waging war against
An enemy as great at this?

BODUICA.

How 'great'?
Think you that Rome can match the peerless pride
Of we who live here? Of my Icenian kin?
Of you and your mighty Trinovantes?

CUNOBELINE.

What would you have me do?

BOUDICA.

I'd have you fight.

CUNOBELINE.

We are too few.

BOUDICA.

Then we shall make us more.

CUNOBELINE.

This is madness.

BOUDICA.

Then madmen we shall seek.
We shall to Badvoc, king of the Belgics.

CUNOBELINE.

What?

BOUDICA.

We need us madmen.

CUNOBELINE.

Aye – but him?
There's madness – then there's Badvoc. He and his kind
Are barely more than animals, who joy
In war and little else.

BOUDICA.

Thus are they perfect
For spilling Roman blood.

CUNOBELINE.

And how will we
Enlist this king?

BOUDICA.

You shall convince him.

CUNOBELINE.

Me?

BOUDICA.

My tongue is an imperfect instrument,
Brusque and coarse, not for diplomacy;
But I have seen you talk so skilfully,
That you could word the sun from out the sky.
How could this king resist your statesman's charms?

CUNOBELINE.

So I'm to make a pact with he my foe?

BOUDICA.

The enemy of my enemy is my friend.

CUNOBELINE.

I still say this is madness.

BOUDICA.

'Tis the times
Which are themselves turned mad.

CUNOBELINE.

P'raps you're right
And it would take a madman to fight them.

BOUDICA.

Or else a woman mad.

CUNOBELINE.

Full right you are.
My sword is yours, fair queen – let us both fight.

BOUDICA.

Oh brave and noble friend, my hearty thanks!
Andraste will herself ensure that you
Are crowned in victory for these your deeds.

CUNOBELINE.

Clothen.

CLOTHEN.

  My lord.

CUNOBELINE.

    Send messengers tonight
To Badvoc. Tell him that we come in peace
To speak of war against a common foe.
We shall ourselves ride at dawn's first light
To meet the king. Go now.

CLOTHEN.

    At once, great king.

 Exeunt.

ACT THREE

Scene One

The camp of GAIUS SUETONIUS, *Anglesey.*

Enter GAIUS SUETONIUS, SOLDIERS *and* DRUID, *bound and bloody.*

SUETONIUS.
Where are your kin, Druid? Speak.

DRUID.
I do not know.

A SOLDIER *strikes the* DRUID.

SUETONIUS.
I said speak.

The DRUID *incants in a low voice.*

What? Soldier, ask him to speak up.

A SOLDIER *strikes the* DRUID *again.*

SOLDIER.
The general said speak up, you filthy piece of shit!

DRUID.
I'll speak no more to him –

SUETONIUS.
You won't if I charge my men cut out your tongue and feed it to the dogs.

DRUID.
– but rather I parlay with the woods.

SUETONIUS.
Oh really? What do the woods say?

DRUID.

They are angered.

SUETONIUS.

With who?

DRUID.

With those who trespass on our land.

SUETONIUS.

This is no longer your land, priest. This is Rome. Now, do not waste my time: where are your kin?

DRUID.

They are not here.

SUETONIUS.

Then where are they?

DRUID.

You will not find them. The woods themselves will hide them from you, bend their boughs and shroud them from your view, twist paths and ways till you are lost, choke you with roots and vines. The gods of these here woods protect us and they will not sleep until they see you and all your men dead.

SUETONIUS *gives a signal to the* SOLDIER. *The* SOLDIER *breaks the* DRUID'*s fingers.*

SUETONIUS.

If you tell us where we can find your camp, I can assure you that we will be merciful in our capture. But if you force my men to traipse through these woods, knee high in thickets and shit, I cannot guarantee that when they find your filthy kin – and make no mistake, they shall – I cannot guarantee that they will not bring down all of Mars' bloodiest works upon you. What do you say?

The DRUID *spits in his face.*

Have him crucified. Nail up a message at his feet in whatever pigshit tongue they speak that so befalls the fate of any who resist the might of Rome.

Exeunt.

Scene Two

The feasting hall of BADVOC.

Enter BOUDICA, BLODWYNN, ALONNA, CUNOBELINE
and BADVOC.

CUNOBELINE.
Well met, great king – we humbly give you thanks
For meeting us. It warms my heart to speak
With you like this, far from the battlefield.

BADVOC.
I liked it more when we did meet in battle.
At least we both knew where we stood.
But come, we'll hear you speak. What is the cause
Of calling on us thus?

CUNOBELINE.
In short: a war.
Not between our kind but rather Rome.
For too long they have plagued our island, dug
Into our coffers, nay the earth itself
And left us hollow. Now we say: no more.
We seek to build an army great enough
To topple Rome's high towers – and humbly beg
That you will join us in our fight to rid
This land of pestilence. Will you join us?

BADVOC.
No.

CUNOBELINE.
No?

BADVOC.
Why should we fight? Rome knows
To leave us well alone. Icenia
Is not my kingdom; its kin are not my kin.
Why should I care what happens there?

BOUDICA.
Because
Icenia's miseries are mirrors of

The woes that will befall your kingdom if
You do not act.

BADVOC.

If Rome dare come
Then we will fight them.

CUNOBELINE.

Why not fight them now?
The best defence is to attack, so let's
Assume advantage of the time, and join
Our forces all as one and make a move
To strike at Rome when they expect it least.

BADVOC.

'Tis not my kingdom's fight. I shall not wade
Into a war that profits not my kin
But only serves to restore this queen her throne.

BOUDICA.

Are you afraid?

BADVOC.

What say you?

BOUDICA.

You heard me.
Are you afraid?

BADVOC.

Badvoc fears no man
Nor woman neither.

BOUDICA.

Then why are you afear'd
To take on Rome?

BADVOC.

Do you hear me now, queen?
I fear not Rome.

BOUDICA.

Then why will you not fight?
I know that more than any of us, you

Do long to lance the bastards on your blade;
And yet, I think deep down you fear one day
That Rome might slip the yoke around your neck,
And make you bend back double for their glee.

BADVOC.
That fate will not befall us.

BOUDICA.
Are you so sure?
We offer you the chance to fight with us –
And if you scorn it, there may come a day,
When Rome stands at your borders, javelins high
And ready to advance; and you will find
All others gone, and you yourself alone,
Toe to toe against an empire's might.
You are a proud and noble king – why then
Should you risk Rome debasing you? Join us.
Bury the hatchet 'tween us – or better still,
Come sink it deep into the flesh of Rome.
What say you, king?

BADVOC.
I say you talk a lot.

BOUDICA.
But I speak the truth.

BADVOC.
Aye – that you do.

BOUDICA.
Well then?

BADVOC.
Know Badvoc – though he holds small love for you,
Or you, Cunobeline – he is no fool.
We must make sure it's Rome, not us, that falls.
I'll lend you arms and men beside.

CUNOBELINE.
Well said,
Oh noble king!

BADVOC.

And Belgic men at that!
Thirty thousand, though you'd hardly need
A single more than one, for you'll not find
A man throughout this isle – nor twenty men –
Who could outdo a Belgic at the blade.

BOUDICA.

Your troops combined with the Trinovantes
And my Icenians makes a fearsome horde
Who'll teach these the Romans how to fear again.

BADVOC.

Where strike we first?

BOUDICA.

At Camulodunum.

BADVOC.

Why not Londinium? Surely there first.
With this one blow, we strike the Roman snake
At this its head.

BOUDICA.

But Camulodunum
While not the seat political, remains
The heart of Roman trade and wealth. Why strike
The head when you can gouge the heart and watch
Your enemy bleed slowly to his death?

BADVOC.

I like this thinking, queen, and were you not
Icenian born, I'd swear you Belgic were.
So, it is settled – come morning, we will rise
And ride us to our kingdoms, there to rouse
Our troops, and then to Camulodunum.
Till then the gods be with you, noble friends –
When next we meet it will be side by side
And with the blood of Rome upon our swords.

Exit BADVOC *and* CUNOBELINE.

BOUDICA.
How now, my girls? Is not this good? Does not
Your heart beat quick with vengeance?

BLODWYNN.

That it does.

BOUDICA.
And you Alonna?

ALONNA.

Mine too.

BOUDICA.

And yet methinks
I see a paleness creeping in your cheeks.

ALONNA.
What if we fail? Though we have heard you speak
Of how Rome's grown complacent, are they not
Still masters of this isle?

BOUDICA.

Do not speak so.
No Roman is your master, nor any man
A lord to you except yourself, my girl –
Though girl I should no longer call you now,
For we must warriors be, not shrinking babes.
Come – show me how you fight. Come. Show me how
A warrior defends what's rightful hers.

ALONNA.
Mother –

BOUDICA *draws and feints at* ALONNA.

ALONNA *draws and parries. They spar.*

BOUDICA.
And will you, Blodwynn, let your sister show
You for a sluggard? Draw your blade and fight!

She feints at BLODWYNN *who draws and parries.*

The three of them spar, the girls trying to best their mother.

BOUDICA *disarms them and holds them both at their swords' tips.*

You have great skill, Alonna – p'raps more than I –
But oh too caring is your heart. It lacks
The fire that should drive your weapon home.
And you, fierce Blodwynn, fight with such a flame
But let your temper get the best of you –
A queen must needs be cool as well as fierce.
If you can conquer these defects, there's none
Who'd raise a blade against you and live to tell it.
D'you understand?

BLODWYNN.
                              We do.

BOUDICA.
                                        Alonna?

ALONNA.
                                                  Aye.

BOUDICA.
You will be royalty yet – but first you must
Take back the kingdom which they wrongly robbed.
Steel your nerve and still your hand, and pray
That sweet Andrasate grant us victory.
Now come: we must prepare our troops. Let's hence.

Exit BOUDICA.

BLODWYNN.
Does not your blood, Alonna, pump so fast
To hear those war drums, thinking how we'll stand
Side by side to strike the heart of Rome?

ALONNA.
It does, my sister.

BLODWYNN.
                    Heard you how she said
We could become such warriors one day?

ALONNA.
I heard her, Blodwynn.

BLODWYNN.
                              Then why look you so?
   This is an honour. We must do her proud.
   Come – fight with me. I needs must practise till
   My sword is quick as hers; till it becomes
   As lightning in my hands.

ALONNA.
                              Some other time.

BLODWYNN.
   Nay, Lo, come spar –

ALONNA.
                              Another time, I said!

BLODWYNN.
   What's this anger?

ALONNA.
   It is not anger that I feel, but fear.
   To ride us into battle, raise the sword
   And spill us blood? My heart quakes at the thought.
   Are you not fearful too?

BLODWYNN.
                              Aye, I am afraid,
   But you heard her – we are no longer babes,
   But warriors, and I one day a queen,
   And I would have no other by my side
   To aid me in my rule than you, sister.

ALONNA.
   My hand still shakes.

BLODWYNN.
                              Then let it rest in mine
   Until such time you calm it with the clasp
   Of sharpened steel. Come, sister, let's away.

   Exeunt.

Scene Three

A gatehouse at Camulodunum.

Three SOLDIERS *on watch –* CATO, LUCIUS *and* SESTUS.

CATO.
　Honey, I think.

SESTUS.
　Oh mercy, gods.

CATO.
　I miss that the most.

LUCIUS.
　They have honey here.

CATO.
　Not like Umbrian honey. Nothing beats the sweetness of that.

SESTUS.
　Sweet Jupiter, if you are merciful, strike me dead –

Enter MESSENGER.

MESSENGER.
　Captain! Captain!

CATO.
　What?

LUCIUS.
　Who goes there?

SESTUS.
　Halt!

MESSENGER.
　A messenger from the Fifth.

LUCIUS.
　Why so hasty?

MESSENGER.
　I must speak with your captain.

CATO.

Have you news?

SESTUS.

Course he has news – he's a fucking messenger.

MESSENGER.

Barbarians. From the north. Thousands –

LUCIUS.

What?

MESSENGER.

Tens of thousands, hundreds – marching in formation, bearing spears and axes, broadswords, chariots, they come – men and women, dipped in paint, bloody and wild – I come to warn – they've overrun our camp.

CATO.

Where are they going?

MESSENGER.

Here.

LUCIUS.

Camulodunum?

SESTUS.

How far are they?

MESSENGER.

A day's ride – maybe less.

LUCIUS.

The gods!

MESSENGER.

Your captain, I must speak with your captain.

Exeunt.

Scene Four

Outside Camulodunum.

Enter BOUDICA, CUNOBELINE *and* BADVOC.

BOUDICA.
  How fare the troops?

BADVOC.
                  My men are set to cleave
  Soft Roman flesh from bone.

CUNOBELINE.
                  And so are mine.
  Though they have marched, they're eager still to fight.

BOUDICA.
  Give word amongst your men, and so to ours
  And all the rest that we rise with the dawn
  And shall before the sun has crowned the sky
  Have brought down hell upon the Roman fiends.

Exit CUNOBELINE *and* BADVOC.

  And bring them hell we shall – or so we must
  Else I have brought this army here for naught.
  'Tis not just me and mine I have enjoined
  Unto this course, but thousands others too,
  A multitude of swords at my command,
  Each every one willing to die for me,
  Their lives all in my hands, their blood – If I
  Do not claim victory today, then all is – No.
  Steel your heart, woman. Be you a queen.

War drums.

Enter the armies of Britain – amassed and massive – with
BOUDICA*'s war chariot.*

She climbs into it and addresses her troops.

  You Britons, hear me! For Britons are we all:
  We are of different tribes, but stand today
  United by a common foe of Rome.

Rome calls us savages – wild, mongrel beasts.
Well – let us show them just how wild we are!

Cheers and battle cries.

Exeunt.

Scene Five

Inside Camulodunum.

The BRITONS *are on the other side of the city gates.*

Enter CENTURION 1 *and* SOLDIERS.

CATO.
The troops have taken positions, sir.

CENTURION 1.
How many are we?

LUCIUS.
Three hundred.

SESTUS.
What the fuck are we supposed to do?

CENTURION 1.
Stand your ground and hold them off. Support will come
from the Procurator. The messenger was swift, our need
great. We will be answered.

SESTUS.
Where did so many of this fucking rabble come from?

War drums and battle cries are heard offstage.

LUCIUS.
Does that sound like a fucking rabble to you?

CENTURION 1.
Order the citizens to stay in their houses. If we are overrun –

More drums and battle cries.

CATO.
  Sweet Jupiter.

CENTURION 1.
  If we are overrun, tell them head to the temple. We can
  protect them there.

  *More war drums and battle cries. The gates heave under the
  weight of the army outside.*

LUCIUS.
  There's thousands.

CENTURION 1.
  Stand your ground.

CATO.
  Sir, the men – I don't think –

CENTURION 1.
  Stand you your ground!

  *War drums and battle cries again. The gates cannot hold any
  longer.*

SESTUS.
  We can't hold them back any longer, sir, we –

CENTURION 1.
  I said stand your fucking –

  Suddenly the gates burst open and the BRITONS *flood in to
  attack the city.*

  *It is as if one hundred years of vengeful anger has been
  released in one instant.*

  Fire, screaming, fighting, blood, chaos – ROMAN TROOPS
  are slaughtered by the hundreds.

  Enter CENTURION 1 *and* SOLDIERS.

CATO.
  They've breached the walls!

CENTURION 1.
Where are the cavalry?

LUCIUS.
We're fucked, we're fucked!

CENTURION 1.
Fall back, fall back!

SESTUS.
Retreat!

Enter BOUDICA, BLODWYNN, ALONNA,
CUNOBELINE, BADVOC *and their armies.*

They fight the ROMANS.

BOUDICA *corners* SESTUS.

Mercy, mercy!

She impales him on her lance.

BOUDICA.
We must not rest until each single soul
Who bears the name of Roman lies them dead
And we have drenched our bodies in their blood.
Now torch the houses! Drive them from their homes!

The BRITONS *set fire to the houses and buildings, the
flames consume the city.*

ROMAN CITIZENS *flee throughout the streets and are cut
down by the* BRITONS.

BLODWYNN *and* ALONNA *chasing two* SOLDIERS,
CATO *and* LUCIUS.

They are cornered by approaching WARRIORS *and
trapped.*

The two sisters attack CATO *and* LUCIUS *and kill them.*

CUNOBELINE.
'Tis ours, great queen – this bloody victory
And this your city is returned to you!

BADVOC *and* BLODWYNN *drag on* CENTURION 1,
bound and bloody, a prisoner.

CENTURION 1.
I beg you, mercy, noble warriors – charity!

BADVOC.
You would have charity?

BLODWYNN.
We'll slit your throat!

CENTURION 1.
Mercy!

ALONNA.
What's going on?

BLODWYNN.
We found this cowering wretch
With tears streamed down his face like a weeping babe.

CENTURION 1.
I beg you, gentlelady, mercy please!

BADVOC.
Silence, wretch – stop your whimpering
And die you like a man.

ALONNA.
The battle's won,
The city's ours, there is no further need
To kill this man.

BADVOC.
What do you talk of 'need'?

ALONNA.
He is unarmed and can do you no harm.

CENTURION 1.
It's true, I mean no harm, I beg you – please!

ALONNA.
There is no need to kill him thus.

BLODWYNN.

No need?

He is a Roman. What more do you need?

BLODWYNN *raises* CENTURION 1*'s weapon to kill him.*

BOUDICA.

Stay your hand!

BLODWYNN.

What say you, Mother?

BADVOC.

You'd show this Roman mercy?

BOUDICA.

Mercy? No,

But Alonna speaks aright: we do not need
To kill this man, but rather shall instead
Find different use for him.

CENTURION 1.

Oh gracious queen!

My thanks, I –

BOUDICA *grabs him by the throat and two* WARRIORS
hold him while she cuts out his tongue.

BOUDICA.

Get you to Catus Deciamus quick
And tell him of what has befallen here.

BADVOC.

How will he tell when he has not a tongue
To tell?

BOUDICA.

Good Badvoc, there are always ways
A man may pass a message without a tongue
To our dear Procurator. But now, come –
We have fought well, so let us claim reward.
Inform the troops that they may take what gold
And prisoners they can find. But do't with haste:
This battle was the first, but there is more

Much more to come – I promise you, my friends.
So fix your javelin tips toward the south
And let us leave this city in the ash
For soon new streets with Roman blood shall run
As we march on and claim Londinium.

Drums.

Blackout.

Interval.

PART TWO: THE FLOOD

ACT FOUR

Scene One

The ruins of Camulodunum.

BOUDICA*'s army are celebrating the destruction of the city.*

They drink and sing a victory song – it's brutal and wild.

THE ARMY.
    We came (we came)
    We came to fight
    To fight the bastards well
    We came to fight, we came to kill
    We came to send them straight to hell!

    Goddess, give me strength, guide the sword in my hand
    We will cut the bastards down, we will win back this land!

    We fought (we fought)
    We fought today
    In rain and filth and mud
    We fought them long, we fought them hard
    We bathed us in the bastards' blood

    Goddess, give me strength, guide the sword in my hand
    We will cut the bastards down, we will win back this land!

    We march (we march)
    We march tomorrow
    We march at dawn's first light
    We march us far, we march us wide
    We march to carry on the fight

    Goddess, give me strength, guide the sword in my hand
    We will cut the bastards down, we will win back this land!

Meanwhile:

Enter SILVIA, *a Roman captive, being chased by two* BELGIC WARRIORS.

SILVIA.
Help! Help!

The WARRIORS *grab* SILVIA.

BELGIC WARRIOR 1.
Shut your mouth.

BELGIC WARRIOR 2.
Hold her.

SILVIA.
Help!

BELGIC WARRIOR 1.
I said shut your fucking mouth, you stupid –

SILVIA *bites the* WARRIOR.

Ah! You fucking –

He strikes her.

Bitch bit me.

BELGIC WARRIOR 2.
Better watch her mouth. Romans got bite on them.

BELGIC WARRIOR 1.
I'll fucking give her mouth something.

They hold her down and prepare to rape her. SILVIA *screams and struggles.*

Enter ALONNA, *who sees the assault on* SILVIA.

ALONNA.
Get away from her!

BELGIC WARRIOR 2.
                Who's that?

ALONNA.

> I said
> Get away, unless you'd have me cleave
> Your cock from 'tween your legs.

BELGIC WARRIOR 1.

> Fuck off, you hear me?

ALONNA.

> And I said let her go.
> You will not sate your rutting with this girl.
> Let go of her or I shall take her from you.

They draw their weapons.

BELGIC WARRIOR 1.

> I'll cut your throat you nosy, fucking bitch!

They attack ALONNA.

She draws her weapon and fights back.

ALONNA *wounds* WARRIOR 1 *then attacks* WARRIOR 2.

Enter BOUDICA, BLODWYNN, BADVOC *and*
CUNOBELINE.

BOUDICA.

> Drop your weapons, lest we should be forced
> To pry them from your bloody hands. Drop them!

They drop their weapons.

> What mischief's here? What are these men about?

BELGIC WARRIOR 1.

> My lord, she attacked us.

BADVOC.

> What?

BELGIC WARRIOR 2.

> Crept up on us, drew her sword –

BELGIC WARRIOR 1.

> Wounded him and meant to murder me –

BADVOC.
This will not stand!

ALONNA.
They meant to rape this girl.

BELGIC WARRIOR 1.
She was our captive.

BELGIC WARRIOR 2.
To do with what we like.

BOUDICA.
And you saw savagery as fit for you?

BELGIC WARRIOR 1.
She's ours, m'lord.

BADVOC.
You'll pay for this, princess –

BOUDICA.
Badvoc, peace!

BADVOC.
She must answer for this.
The honour of my men has been abused –

ALONNA.
Honour? 'Mongst these savages?

BADVOC.
There must
Be satisfaction for these words.

ALONNA.
They were
The first to draw.

BOUDICA.
Did you invite her fight?

BELGIC WARRIOR 1.
Well, yes – We drew us first, but only cos –

BOUDICA.
Then witness, Badvoc, she did not attack
But rather did defend herself against
Their blows –

BADVOC.
But she did claim their property
Which you yourself decreed was free to loot.
What: may she now tell my men what to do
With these their goods?

ALONNA.
Is this the world, Mother,
You'd have us fight for? Where girls are naught but meat
To sate the hunger of such savage beasts?

BELGIC WARRIOR 1.
You meddling bitch!

ALONNA.
You want some more?

BOUDICA.
Enough!
We'll have us no more fighting. Badvoc, go
And take your men to surgeons straight, and take
This girl with them.

ALONNA.
Mother, do not do this!

BELGIC WARRIOR 1.
She is our property!

BELGIC WARRIOR 2.
She's ours!

ALONNA.
Mother, please!

BADVOC.
The girl is theirs – you shall not take their loot.

BOUDICA.

    Then I shall buy her. Blodwynn, pay these men
    With gold from our reserves – and make it double.
    I'm nothing if not generous.

BLODWYNN.

                         You're not
    About to waste our gold on this one girl?

ALONNA.

    Blodwynn –

BLODWYNN.

              'Tis madness! Badvoc, keep you the girl –

BOUDICA.

    Blodwynn –

BLODWYNN.

             – she is your men's. We shall not waste
    A single coin of ours upon –

BOUDICA.

                  Blodwynn!
    The order has been given.

BADVOC.

                It is not yours to give.

BOUDICA.

    This is my army, Badvoc.

BADVOC.

             And these my men!
    You will not treat them thus –

CUNOBELINE.

             Enough now, peace!
    We have, my friends, enjoyed a victory
    And struck a mighty blow against foul Rome.
    We should be celebrating, joining arms,
    Not squabbling for spoils like greedy children.
    We are united, are we not? Let us

> Behave as such, forget these petty strifes
> And focus now how we may make the most
> Of this success; on what we shall do next.
> Are we agreed?

BADVOC.
> You're lucky, queen, our victory has put
> King Badvoc in a generous mood. We shall
> Withdraw – though we do not forgive,
> Nor certainly forget, what happened here.

> *Exit* BADVOC *and the* BELGIC WARRIORS.

CUNOBELINE.
> Give Badvoc time – no doubt he'll soon forget
> This incident. I should attend my troops,
> Toast our success and plan what's yet to come.

> *Exit* CUNOBELINE.

BOUDICA.
> Blodwynn.

> BLODWYNN *goes to* BOUDICA.

> BOUDICA *strikes her.*

> Do not dare to undermine me
> Before our allies. Is that understood?

BLODWYNN.
> But –

BOUDICA.
> Is that understood?

BLODWYNN.
> Yes.

BOUDICA.
> Good.
> Now get you gone – and fetch Badvoc his gold.

> BLODWYNN *exits.*

> What means this, child? Have you gone mad withal?

ALONNA.

   Not mad, dear Mother, rather sick with grief
   That we allow such men as these to roam
   And call them fellow soldiers in our fight.

BOUDICA.

   We needs must have these men, or else we can
   No longer hope to bring down mighty Rome.

ALONNA.

   In having such as these, we do become
   As beasts ourselves.

BOUDICA.

               Then beasts we will become
   If that is what it takes to reclaim our home.
   We march at dawn, I've much to see to. Go.
   Take your slave and get you from my sight.

   Exit BOUDICA.

   ALONNA *approaches* SILVIA.

ALONNA.

   Do not be frightened. I will not harm you. Come –
   We shall retire and attend your wounds.
   I bid you – come.

   Exeunt.

Scene Two

Londinium.

The palace of CATUS DECIAMUS.

Enter CATUS *with* SEJANUS.

CATUS.
How can this be? A pack of mongrel apes
Have bested us?

SEJANUS.
My lord –

CATUS.
'My lord' me not,
Sejanus – I am sick with this your news.
Send you westward word towards Suetonius.
We needs must have him here at once.

Enter SOLDIER *carrying* CENTURION 1 – *broken and
limp in tattered, bloody clothes.*

SOLDIER.
My lord!

CATUS.
What is this man?

SOLDIER.
'Tis Marcellus Sextus, leader of the Eighth at
Camulodunum. We found him lain half-dead at the gate, sir.

CATUS.
What happened to the city? What men survive?
Captain, speak! What army do we face?

CENTURION 1 *tries to speak, but all that comes out is
tongueless, guttural moans and streams of blood.*

SOLDIER.
When we came to dress his wounds, we found this too.

He removes the CENTURION*'s uniform to reveal on his
back a message carved into the flesh with a knife: 'DEATH
TO ROME'.*

CATUS.
Who sent this?

SOLDIER.
Sir, it was Queen Boudica.

CATUS.
You're telling me this – woman came and killed
All of our men, crushed Camulodunum
And slaughtered all its citizens?

SOLDIER.
Oh no,
She is no woman, sir, but something worse.
Report is Hell itself, fearing her wrath
Had spat her out again upon the earth –
She did appear belike a Fury, eyes
Full-brim with venom, hair wild serpentine
And bearing bloody vengeance in both hands.

CATUS.
Go get you gone – forewarn the troops, tell them
Prepare themselves for battle. Go now. Go!

Exit all except CATUS.

This queen intends to murder me, and shall
Tear down this isle entire till she's writ
In Death's own mortal book my name in blood.
What should I then? Why – must I stay and fight?
Am I to die so he the Emperor
May keep this squalid rock while he just sits
Like a pig in shit in Rome's own hallowed halls?
I know 'tis cowardly for soldiers thus
To flee when they should stay and face the foe
And die an honest Roman death; but I
Am not a soldier. Death brings me no fame.
If I die here, no glories shall be sung
To me, no one will weep. They will
But say 'Oh, how unfortunate' then send
Some other poor, pathetic pencil-pusher
To take my place as though I never existed.

I needs must fly this godforsaken isle
And find my refuge elsewhere. I'll to Gaul
And house me with my kinfolk there until
This carnage passes. Do not look at me
Like that. There's none of you who'd stay – or if
They say they would, they are an idiot.
Call me a coward; a liar if you must
But let it not be said I am a fool.

Exit CATUS.

Scene Three

BOUDICA*'s camp – a day's march from Londinium.*

Inside ALONNA*'s tent,* SILVIA *is waiting.*

Enter ALONNA.

ALONNA.
Don't be startled. It's only me. I brought
Some food for you – I thought you ought to eat.
How are your injuries?

SILVIA.
                    They are better.

ALONNA.
I'm glad to hear it. Let me have a look.
They're healing well. The dressing needs a change.

She tends to SILVIA*'s wounds.*

SILVIA.
What is that which you spread beneath the gauze?

ALONNA.
An unction that will help your wounds to heal.
Already it has worked a marvel – see?

SILVIA.
What's in it?

ALONNA.
                Several woodland herbs and blooms,
    Unremarkable to untrained eyes,
    But which possess great medicine to those
    Who speak their language.

SILVIA.
                        And who taught you their tongue?

ALONNA.
    My mother taught me, and she herself did learn
    From great Andraste, goddess of victory –
    Or so she told me when I was a girl.

SILVIA.
    My husband was a man of physic too.
    He too could conjure medicines that healed
    The sick and made the body whole.
    He was a man of wondrous learning, kind
    And full of caring.

ALONNA.
                Where is your husband now?

SILVIA.
    Amidst the ashes at Camulodunum.

ALONNA.
    Come – eat your food. You must build your strength.

SILVIA.
    How fare your comrades' injuries?

ALONNA.
                        Comrades?

SILVIA.
    Your fellows that were injured in the fight.

ALONNA.
    Those men were not my kind – I do not owe
    Allegiance to such savages.

SILVIA.

I thought –

ALONNA.

We were the same? I wouldn't worry. You
All look the same to us – all soft and smooth.
I wonder how you can survive the cold.
But you were lucky to escape. 'Tis said
The Belgics sport in torture. Icenia
Would not debase her prisoners so. If we
Did treat them thus, we'd be no better than
These brutes, or worse still Rome.

SILVIA.

What has Rome done

To you?

ALONNA.

Rome has injured me.

SILVIA.

Then why save me?

ALONNA.

You never did me wrong.

SILVIA.

Nor did my husband. Nor did anyone
Who lived at Camulodunum. I saw
A boy of five or so that was cut down
As he did flee his dying mother's arms.
Was he the Rome that did you injury?

ALONNA.

Rome took my home from me.

SILVIA.

You took mine.

ALONNA.

This is my land. I was born here.

SILVIA.

Me too.

I was not born but thirty miles from here.
I've never known of any other place.
I met my husband here; had hoped to raise
My children too.

ALONNA.
                        But what of Rome?

SILVIA.
                                    What's 'Rome'?
Rome's just a word to me – this is my home.

Enter BLODWYNN.

BLODWYNN.
    Sister.

ALONNA.
            What is it, Blodwynn?

BLODWYNN.
                            Our mother calls.

ALONNA.
    I'll come when I am finished.

BLODWYNN.
                            She bade you leave
Whatever – little business you attend
And come immediately.

ALONNA.
                    Alright. I come.

BLODWYNN.
    Do not take long – our mother bid us haste.

Exit BLODWYNN.

ALONNA.
    Your wounds are dressed – you ought to rest you now.
    Leave not this tent if you value your life.

SILVIA.
    Am I your prisoner?

ALONNA.

Get you some rest. We'll speak more in the morn.

SILVIA.

What is your name? You never told me.

ALONNA.

My name's Alonna.

SILVIA.

I am Silvia.

ALONNA.

Well – goodnight, Silvia.

SILVIA.

Goodnight to you.

Exit ALONNA.

Scene Four

BOUDICA*'s camp – inside* BOUDICA*'s tent.*

Enter BOUDICA *and* CUNOBELINE.

BOUDICA.

And can he not come here himself and speak?

CUNOBELINE.

The king is proud and demands you go to him.
I warned you when you bid me bring him in
To this our cause –

BOUDICA.

And did you tell me not
'Give Badvoc time – no doubt he'll soon forget'?
Your auguries are marvellous, Cunobeline.

CUNOBELINE.

Think you it easy to play the go-between
With you and Badvoc?

BOUDICA.

No one asked you.

CUNOBELINE.

No,
But still it is a role I must endure
If we are to succeed –

Enter ALONNA *and* BLODWYNN.

ALONNA.

You called for us.
Should we wait –

CUNOBELINE.

No, you ought to stay, for this
Concerns you too, or rather what you did
To Badvoc's men –

ALONNA.

I would not call them 'men'.

CUNOBELINE.

Well, men or no, we need them for our fight,
And if you, princess, slander this their name
In quarrel with them, you threaten this our cause
And undermine your mother's rule –

BOUDICA.

Think you,
Cunobeline, I am not fit to lead
This army sans the aid of men? I can
Speak for myself. If I need help, I'll ask.

CUNOBELINE.

You did ask me – the night you bid me join
Your fight.

BOUDICA.

'Tis your fight too. 'Tis all our fight.
Bid you remember that –

CUNOBELINE.

And bid you, queen,

Remember that I am a king, and friend.
I'd have you speak to me as such –

BOUDICA.

                 And I
Would have you trust my judgement. Take me not
To be a girl unschooled in queenly rule.
Trust me. Now – I'd kindly ask your leave.
I'd like to speak in private with my kin.
And worry not – I shall to Badvoc talk
And smooth these choppy waters.

CUNOBELINE.

                 Very well –
But be advised there're more rough seas ahead
And not from just your enemy, my friend.

Exit CUNOBELINE.

BOUDICA.
Bid you leave as well, Blodwynn. I'd have
Some words with she your sister.

BLODWYNN.

                What – must I go?
Whatever you have to say to her, you can
Say so in front of me.

BOUDICA.

           I'd speak with her
And her alone. There's issue to be had.
I ask you, Blodwynn – give us leave awhile.
I shall come seek you out later tonight.

BLODWYNN *exits*.

ALONNA.
What would you, Mother?

BOUDICA.

          Pray you, girl, be still.
I see the tempests in your eyes, and hear
Your words like weapons levelled 'gainst our friends.

ALONNA.
Our friends are fools.

BOUDICA.
                              Speak you of Cunobeline?

ALONNA.
This foolish king sees virtue in a cur
And takes brutality for bravery.

BOUDICA.
This 'foolish king' is your better, girl,
Commanding armies, fighting wars when you
Were but a babe-in-arms. When you have ruled
As long as he – When you are one day queen,
Then may you question him.

ALONNA.
                              You'd have me queen?
But what of Blodwynn? The throne is hers by right –

BOUDICA.
Blodwynn is bold and fiery, a gifted blade,
A fearsome warrior, no one can doubt –
But she's no more than a fighter; she has not
The gift of leadership I see in you.
The foresight, care or cunning; she has not
The wisdom that her people sorely need
To raise Icenia from the dark again.
'Tis for our kingdom's sake I crown you queen.
Speak, Lo – is not this good?

ALONNA.
                              Aye, Mother.

BOUDICA.
                                        And yet?

ALONNA.
Pray, Mother, I am honoured you should choose
Myself to lead our people – but I confess,
I have me –

BOUDICA.

What? You have you what?

ALONNA.

I have me doubts.

BOUDICA.
Doubts? What doubts?

ALONNA.

If this is our best course.

BOUDICA.
What would you have?

ALONNA.

I'd have you cease this fight.
The Romans are in flight; their scattered troops
Are flung unto the winds; there is report
That he the Procurator's fled to Gaul.
We have the power – what need we spill more blood?
Rather we can parlay now with Rome
And so secure our freedoms and our lands
With no more bloodshed –

BOUDICA.

Do you hear yourself?
You ask me to show mercy to the men
Who slew my people, beat my body, stole
My kingdom, without saying what they did
To you, my daughter, on that fateful night –

ALONNA.
I need me no reminders!

BOUDICA.

Yet you beg
Compassion for these monsters?

ALONNA.

They were not,
Those women, men and children – which we slew
In thousands in the city streets – monsters.
They were but humble people.

BOUDICA.

They were Rome
And as such they were monstrous.

ALONNA.

What then are you
Who slaughters babes-in-arms if not monstrous?
I beg you: talk with Rome and sue for peace.

BOUDICA.

I can't do that.

ALONNA.

You can't or won't?

BOUDICA.

I won't.
Why should I throw aside what we have won?
Why else have I done this if not for you?
Go get you gone, but I expect to see
You by my side tomorrow with your sword
Ready to lead your people 'gainst the city.

ALONNA.

I'll be there at your side – but hope my plea
May turn your heart from hell toward the light.

Exit ALONNA.

BOUDICA.

You simple girl – can you not see the gears
Of war are turning, whether I will or no?
This army is in motion. I must walk
Before it as its leader; if I stop
I shall be crushed beneath its marching feet.
Goddess Andraste, please – I beg of you:
Grant me the strength to marshal these wild troops
Before we turn and tear ourselves apart.

Exit BOUDICA.

Scene Five

The palace of CATUS DECIAMUS, *Londinium*.

Enter SUETONIUS *and* CENTURION 2.

SUETONIUS.
    When did this news come?

CENTURION 2.
    Yesterday, sir. They march here to Londinium as we speak.

SUETONIUS.
    How long till they arrive?

CENTURION 2.
    Two days, three at most.

SUETONIUS.
    Mars be my guide – where is the Procurator?

Enter SEJANUS.

SEJANUS.
    He's gone!

SUETONIUS.
            Who's gone?

SEJANUS.
                    The Procurator's fled!
    His rooms are empty, coffers bare, his trunks
    Are packed and gone, there is no trace of him.
    All that remains was this here note that reads
    He's taken refuge with his kin in Gaul.

SUETONIUS.
    Foul, debasing coward! Why has he flown?

SEJANUS.
    He must have flown on hearing it was she
    Who came now hither, searching for his blood.

SUETONIUS.
    Who's she?

SEJANUS.
>Queen Boudica, the Icenian Queen.

SUETONIUS.
>A woman leads this rebellion?

SEJANUS.
>If you can call her a woman, sir – she is
>A dark avenging succubus who broke
>The walls of Camulodunum and now
>Comes here to seal our fate!

SUETONIUS.
>Be silent, fool!
>Unless you'll have me silence you instead?
>How many are we?

CENTURION 2.
>Three thousand, sir –

SUETONIUS.
>And they?

CENTURION 2.
>A hundred thousand, sir.

SUETONIUS.
>It cannot be fought. We shall be overrun and torn to shreds if
>we stay. Centurion, give the order; we strike from
>Londinium and march the troops north-west tonight.

SEJANUS.
>What?

SUETONIUS.
>Give word Marcus Phillipus meet us there with
>reinforcements from the Fifteenth –

SEJANUS.
>But what of this our city?

SUETONIUS.
>The city's dead
>Only the gods could save it. Now, go inform

The citizens of our intents, and bid
They do likewise if they value their lives.

SEJANUS.
That's it?

SUETONIUS.
      That's it.

SEJANUS.
          You can't be serious! You damn
Our city to destruction, tail between
Your quivering legs just like our Procurator!

SUETONIUS.
Watch your tongue! I do not flee, you fool,
But go so that we may fight them again.
I've given you fair warning. Now spread the word
To all the citizens that, come tonight,
They must abandon all or risk their lives

SEJANUS.
The citizens will never leave their home.

SUETONIUS.
Then they must needs be buried here with them.

Exit SUETONIUS *and* CENTURION 2.

In the distance, the sound of war drums approach.

Exit SEJANUS.

Scene Six

A street in Londinium.

The BRITONS *are destroying the city and murdering its inhabitants.*

Enter a ROMAN WOMAN, *clothes torn and stained with ash.*

ROMAN WOMAN.
    Marcus! Marcus! Have you seen my boy?
    I had him with me just a moment ago,
    Holding my hand – he held my hand so tight –
    I told him 'Don't let go, no matter what!'
    But we were pulled apart inside the crowds
    As we were running blindly through the streets
    And now I don't know where to find him –

A sudden deafening noise offstage of battle and bloodshed.

    I saw them, they – their faces caked in blood –
    They looked like – monsters – screaming bloody –

Another noise.

    We ran into the forum, tried to hide,
    But they were waiting, they – They cut us down –
    Everyone, they – They grabbed – They grabbed the girls,
    Little girls, they threw them on the ground and they – they –

Another noise.

    Please, have you seen him? Where is he? Please, where is he?
      Please!
    We have to do something! Don't sit and fucking stare!
    What are you looking at? Why won't you help?
    For god's sake, please, I have to find him – please!

Another noise as two WARRIORS *rush onto the stage, followed by* ALONNA *and* BLODWYNN.

The two WARRIORS *grab the* ROMAN WOMAN *and hold her as she kicks and screams for dear life.*

BLODWYNN *comes up and drives her blade into the*
ROMAN WOMAN'*s belly, then lets her dead body fall to*
the floor.

The WARRIORS *drag off the body.* BLODWYNN *follows*
while ALONNA *remains.*

She waits until they are gone before she doubles over and
vomits.

ALONNA *tries to gather herself, while* BLODWYNN
re-enters, at first unnoticed by her.

BLODWYNN.
So – this is what a queen looks like?

ALONNA.

…

BLODWYNN.

…

ALONNA.
I did not choose this –

BLODWYNN.

And yet she gave it you.
And you did take it. And come tomorrow all
Will know that you are queen and I am not.
Are you not satisfied?

ALONNA.

How can I be?
This blood for blood is madness – it is not right,
It is not just –

BLODWYNN.

Just?

ALONNA.

– this murder is not fair –

BLODWYNN.
This here is war, sister. There is no place for 'fair'.
We could now slay a dozen cities so –

A hundred, and it still would not be 'fair'.
Nor will it be truly 'fair' till we have chased
These murdering bastards back to Rome itself
And visited upon them every year
Of this our slavery; nor will't be 'fair'
Till we have stole each coin they stole from us;
Defiled each inch of land that they defiled;
And finally and 'fairly' paid them back
Each single scar that they have given us. Then
And only then, I think, would it be 'fair'.

ALONNA.

I cannot understand you any more –

BLODWYNN.

What need you 'understand'? I have not changed.
I am the sister learnt to fight with you.
To draw a bow. To ride. To wield a blade.
I am she still – but what are you, sister?
You are our mother's choice. Now act like it –
Or if you are afraid, there's others who
Would lead instead. I love you, Lo –
Just as we shared a womb, we have shared wounds
And I would march into the mouth of hell
For you and for our cause. Would you do so?

Exit BLODWYNN.

*Offstage we hear the sound off war drums and fighting, the
screams of unarmed men, women and children being
slaughtered.*

ALONNA *waits. Listens.*

Exit ALONNA.

ACT FIVE

Scene One

Wattling Road – the camp of GAIUS SUETONIUS.

Inside GAIUS SUETONIUS*'s tent.*

Enter GAIUS SUETONIUS.

SUETONIUS.
    The word that comes from Londinium is death;
    Just as it was with Camulodunum
    And this morning from Verulanium.
    Three cities has this warrior queen cut down
    And now she comes to Wattling Road to seek
    Her further blood. I told my officers
    That we must show no fear against this 'dam
    But stand like plated Mars and give her hell.
    But even as I spoke these words, I thought
    My men could hear them not because my heart
    Did beat so fearfully within my breast
    That it would drown me out and would betray
    The dreadful truth: I am afraid.
    We are outnumbered ten to one; my men
    Are scared and ill-prepared; what's more than all,
    This warrior queen has vengeance in her heart,
    A fire so consuming and so bright
    I fear my eyes will burn to look on it.
    I've battled barbarous hordes and faced me foes
    That would shrink most men's hearts, and barely flinched;
    But she?

    Enter SOLDIER.

SOLDIER.
    Sir.

SUETONIUS.
What is it?

SOLDIER.
There's someone here to see you.

SUETONIUS.
I'm not to be disturbed.

SOLDIER.
She insisted.

SUETONIUS.
She?

SOLDIER.
Yes, sir. A Briton, came upon the gate in plainest sight,
unarmed, alone.

SUETONIUS.
Show her in.

Exit SOLDIER.

She is so bold to come here unprotected?
Perhaps this queen has come withal
To taunt me 'fore the battle.

Enter ALONNA.

You come unto my camp alone. No guard,
Nor neither weapon.

ALONNA.

                I come not here to fight.

SUETONIUS.
Why come you then, O queen?

ALONNA.
I'm not the woman who you take me for.
I am Alonna, Icenia's princess.
My mother Boudica is titled queen.

SUETONIUS.
But, princess as you are, your mother sends
Her daughter here with neither guard nor blade?

ALONNA.
She did not send me.

SUETONIUS.
You come here on your own?
What is your purpose?

ALONNA.
Nothing more than peace.

SUETONIUS.
Your mother sues for peace?

ALONNA.
She neither craves
Nor offers it.

SUETONIUS.
What mean you then?

ALONNA.
I mean
To parlay here with you and find a way
To swiftly bring this bloody conflict's end.

SUETONIUS.
You've lost me.

ALONNA.
Pray then, listen carefully:
Tomorrow you and she intend to fight,
But whosoe'er shall win, we both do lose.
For if we steep this isle into the inks
Of war, the dye shall be forever set
And never shall the stain of death be cleansed.

SUETONIUS.
Why seek you peace?

ALONNA.

                       Though I myself have been
A victim of Rome's savagery; though I
Have been – abused and left for dead; though I
Have suffered at your soldiers' lustful hands,
No better are my army's frightful deeds
As ordered by my mother's own command.
I should delight in this revenge; wallow
In this your blood that we have spilt; but I
Am sick with vengeance. 'Tis a malady
That feeds its victim as it hungers them
So they are never truly satisfied
Even as they gorge themselves to death.
So is it with us both – this war shan't end
Till we down arms and parlay.

SUETONIUS.

                       And you think
That I will parlay with you?

ALONNA.

                    I do think
That though a soldier, you still value life
And do not wish to send men to their deaths.
I beg you: offer peace; give back this isle;
Restore what you have taken from our land;
And I will likewise bargain for your lives
And to my mother plead your case for you
And will ensure you leave here free of harm.
There need be no more bloodshed.

SUETONIUS.

                      I cannot
Offer that which is not mine to give.
This land belongs to Rome and not to me.

ALONNA.

The Procurator's fled – command is yours,
If you but speak then Rome must surely hear.

SUETONIUS.
I am a soldier – my only language war
I do betray my tongue to speak of peace.

ALONNA.
You will not listen?

SUETONIUS.
Will not? I cannot.
I'm bound to fight your mother on the morn.

ALONNA.
Then we have lost.

SUETONIUS.
You may win.

ALONNA.
'Tis not just me
And mine of which I speak – but of us all.

SUETONIUS.
My men will here escort you to the gate
From thereon out, you're on your own, princess.

ALONNA.
Farewell, Suetonius – I truly hope
That when you meet my mother on the morn
The gods show equal mercy to you both.

Exeunt.

Scene Two

BOUDICA*'s camp.*

Enter BOUDICA, CUNOBELINE *and* BADVOC.

BOUDICA.
    Badvoc, I will not stand for these your mad
    And rabid troops who flout my rule –

BADVOC.
                                        I'll not
    Have you call my men mad when we have seen
    What madness you and those your girls –

BOUDICA.
                                        Speak not
    A word about my kin –

BADVOC.
                        Oh, I shall speak
    Howe'er I please –

BOUDICA.
                    You pig!

BADVOC.
                        You bitch!

CUNOBELINE.
                            Enough!
    Our enemy is here upon us, and you
    Are bickering and whining –

BADVOC.
                            Oh, shut your mouth!
    The only voice I'm sick of more than hers
    Is yours, you creeping, spineless shit. You are
    Forever fawning, playing politic –

CUNOBELINE.
    We must together –

BADVOC.
                    Don't tell me what I must.
    I'll do as I will do –

BOUDICA.
                    Don't waste your breath
On such as a fool as this.

BADVOC.
                         I warn you, queen –

Enter BLODWYNN.

BLODWYNN.
  Mother!

BOUDICA.
        Hold you, Blodwynn.

BLODWYNN.
                    Alonna's gone!

BOUDICA.
  Gone? What gone?

BLODWYNN.
                 She's no more in our camp
But fled last night.

BADVOC.
                 And now we see how brave
Your kin are, Boudica.

BOUDICA.
                    Where is she gone?

BLODWYNN.
  Two guards did see her heading north of here.

CUNOBELINE.
  Toward the Roman camp?

BADVOC.
                    The traitorous bitch
Has turned and seeks out favour with our foe
By offering our lives in place of hers.

BOUDICA.
  It is not so.

BLODWYNN.

> The guards have sworn it is

CUNOBELINE.

> O Boudica, what has your daughter done?

BADVOC.

> I bid you: mark this woman and her kin
> For they will drive our army to ruin.

BOUDICA.

> I am still general here, do not forget.

BADVOC.

> And see what discipline you do command
> When even these your girls will not obey.

BOUDICA.

> Shut your mouth, you stinking piece of shit!

BADVOC.

> Look you, Cunobeline, she thinks herself
> A greater majesty than either of us,
> Though till we offered aid to her, she was
> A queen without a kingdom.

BOUDICA.

> I tell you –

BADVOC.

> No!
> You shall tell me no more, queen. We are through.
> You order you your men, and I will mine
> And then we will upon the battlefield witness
> Which of us earns the spoils of victory.
> And I would bid you too, Cunobeline,
> Come out from hiding 'neath your lady's skirts
> Or are the apron strings too tight? Be careful, king,
> For they are like to strangle you one day.

Exit BADVOC.

BOUDICA.

> The stupid bastard – he'll be the death of us!

CUNOBELINE.
Boudica –

BOUDICA.
Well, if he wants to fight
And see whose army is the greatest –

CUNOBELINE.
Boudica!
This charge is serious.

BOUDICA.
'Tis naught but rumour –

CUNOBELINE.
Alonna has betrayed us! And if you don't
Report the deed and here disown her, then
This rumour sure must seep throughout the camp
And poison you, my friend –

BOUDICA.
What friend are you
That bids me damn my daughter to the world?

CUNOBELINE.
The only one that you have left! The rest
Have been driven away by your damn pride,
While I remain – a fool to do so, but
A loyal fool.

BOUDICA.
Then, fool, be gone – no more.

CUNOBELINE.
If you push me away, you do begin
The splint'ring of our cause, which can't be fixed
Nor joined again if it is rent asunder.
I beg you think –

BOUDICA.
And I do bid you go,
And speak you not a word of what's occurred.
Ready your men, await your orders. I
Will meet you on the battlefield anon.

CUNOBELINE.
> I once would follow you to hell's own heart
> And as your equal stand side by side in war.
> But now I see I'm but your instrument,
> And shall be played whether I will or no.

Exit CUNOBELINE.

BLODWYNN.
> Mother, have you gone mad?

BOUDICA.
> Speak not, my child,
> Already I know what you have to say,
> And do not call me 'Mother' thus.

BLODWYNN.
> Well then,
> Call me not 'child', for you are not my 'dam
> Nor cannot be – she would not act this way.

BOUDICA.
> What say you, girl?

BLODWYNN.
> My mother would not base
> Herself so low in blessing traitors thus,
> Nor curse her noble fellows, threaten our cause
> And rent her army favouring a snake.

BOUDICA.
> Speak not this way about your sister –

BLODWYNN.
> She
> Is not my sister any more, but shall
> A stranger to my heart remain.

BOUDICA.
> Blodwynn,
> She is your blood.

BLODWYNN.
> She is my enemy,
> And she is rightly yours.

BOUDICA.
                              I cannot hate
One which I loved so well.

BLODWYNN.
                              She loves you not,
Or else she would not have betrayed you so.
I beg you: cast this traitor to the dust
And bear you like a queen, a warrior
And not a mewling mother –

BOUDICA.
                              Am I not both?
Should I not love my daughter?

BLODWYNN.
                              What has she done
That makes you love her so?

BOUDICA.
                              You are no mother,
Or else you would not speak so heartlessly
About the child you bore –

BLODWYNN.
                              You bore us both!
The two of us are of your soil – and yet
She gets to blossom in your loving sun
While I am left to wither in the shade.

BOUDICA.
Enough, Blodwynn –

BLODWYNN.
                              Why her, not me?

BOUDICA.
                                        Enough!
I am your queen and general. Do you forget?

BLODWYNN.
How could I when I'm ever treated thus:
A soldier, nothing more. Your majesty.

Exit BLODWYNN.

BOUDICA.
How have I made my darling daughters so?
The one so hard that she would slay her sister;
That sister now so soft that she would love
Her foe above her kin. What have I done?

Enter WARRIOR WOMAN.

WARRIOR WOMAN.

My queen.

BOUDICA.
What is it now?

WARRIOR WOMAN.
A message comes from Rome.
Their general asks you lay you down your sword,
And in return he swears Rome shall forgive
These trespasses.

BOUDICA.
What think you we should do?

WARRIOR WOMAN.
What – me, my queen?

BOUDICA.
Do you see any else?

WARRIOR WOMAN.
'Tis not my place to tell my general
How she should lead her army –

BOUDICA.
And yet I ask:
What would you do if you were in my place?

WARRIOR WOMAN.
I'd fight.

BOUDICA.
You would?

WARRIOR WOMAN.

>Of course, your majesty.

BOUDICA.

Do you not fear your life?

WARRIOR WOMAN.

>Why should I fear?

My queen will lead the charge. I need not fear.
If she but tells me fight, then fight I shall.

BOUDICA.

Very well – go tell the Romans thus.
Ready the troops, and then go you prepare
My armour for the battle.

WARRIOR WOMAN.

>At once, my queen.

Exit MESSENGER.

BOUDICA.

I know what I must do, but I cannot
Denounce you, daughter, though my nation cracks
And loving you will ruin us. 'Tis said
To love your children too much is a fault;
But 'tis a fault I willingly commit.

Exit BOUDICA.

Scene Three

The battlefield at Wattling Road.

Enter SUETONIUS *and* CENTURION 2.

CENTURION 2.
    She has refused our call to lay down arms.

SUETONIUS.
    Then we must fight. Give the order to hold fast between
    these high cliff walls and the thick forest. Do not advance,
    but wait till they have come. Their numbers funnelled
    between these cliffs and trees will hamper them. We will
    here defend ourselves until it is our advantage to attack.
    Hold positions. Do not break rank. And bid the gods find
    favour in our deeds.

Exit SUETONIUS *and* CENTURION 2.

War drums.

The two armies appear bearing arms and banners.

The BRITONS *attack.*

It feels like the battle might crack the island in half.

Enter BOUDICA *and* BLODWYNN.

BOUDICA.
    Send messengers to Badvoc – bid him hold
    His army till we've cleared a path. Avaunt!

Exit BOUDICA *and* BLODWYNN.

Enter SUETONIUS *and* CENTURION 2.

CENTURION 2.
    Their forces press upon on us but are crushed by their
    own men.

SUETONIUS.
    Keep them hemmed in – don't give them ground to fight.
    Advance slowly, keep pushing them back!

Exit SUETONIUS *and* CENTURION 2.

Enter BADVOC.

BADVOC.
Let's drive these bastards back. All men – attack!

BADVOC *and his men charge into the fray – noise and chaos.*

Enter BOUDICA *and* BLODWYNN.

BLODWYNN.
We can't break their formations.

BOUDICA.
                              Then pull back.

BLODWYNN.
We're pressed in on all sides, there's no retreat!
Badvoc has pinioned us, and Cunobeline
Has been ensnared and fights now for his life.

Exit BOUDICA *and* BLODWYNN.

Enter CUNOBELINE *and* CLOTHEN.

CUNOBELINE.
Undone, undone, our forces are undone!

CLOTHEN.
My lord, we must go quickly!

CUNOBELINE.
                              What's the use?
The Romans press upon us from the front
And likewise do our troops press from the rear
Till we are crushed and choked here in between.

Enter ROMAN SOLDIERS.

CLOTHEN.
Protect the king!

ROMAN SOLDIER.
Attack!

They fight. CLOTHEN *is killed.* CUNOBELINE *is surrounded.*

CUNOBELINE.
Come on, you bastards!

They fight. CUNOBELINE *is killed.*

Exit ROMAN SOLDIERS.

Enter BOUDICA *and* BLODWYNN.

BLODWYNN.
Our men are lost, our army cracked and broke,
The day is hopeless.

BOUDICA.
                    Come, we must fall back!

BLODWYNN.
We cannot, Mother – our forces still march on
Blocking any chance of our escape.

Enter BADVOC.

BOUDICA.
Badvoc! What have you done?

BADVOC.
                              Have you seen
Cunobeline? He was cut down.

BLODWYNN.
                          Cut down?

BADVOC.
They slit his throat as though he were a hog –
My men are dead or fled – There's no one left –

Enter CENTURION 2 *and* ROMAN SOLDIERS.

BOUDICA.
Retreat unto the forest!

BOUDICA *and* BLODWYNN *exit.*

BADVOC *tries to follow but is surrounded.*

BADVOC.

Come at me, sons of whores, I'll take you all!

They fight. He manages to slay some ROMANS.

Enter GAIUS SUETONIUS.

And will you have me too, you Roman fuck?
Come fight!

They fight. SUETONIUS *kills* BADVOC.

CENTURION 2.

They're retreating!

SUETONIUS.

Where is the queen? Where is she?

CENTURION 2.

Some savages have been spotted making for the forest – 'tis
thought Queen Boudica is there amongst them.

SUETONIUS.

Bring me my horse and to your mounts with hounds, into the
woods and in pursuit. Our quarry is the queen!

Exeunt.

Scene Four

The forest.

Enter BOUDICA, BLODWYNN *and* WARRIORS *in flight.*

The sound of a party of ROMAN SOLDIERS *can be heard –*
horses, hounds, shouting.

BOUDICA.
Where are they?

WARRIOR 1.
                    Right behind us.

WARRIOR 2.
                                    They dog our heels.

BLODWYNN.
Let's make a stand! We shan't go easily,
But take as many of the bastards with us.

BOUDICA.
No, you needs must fly.

BLODWYNN.
                        We needs must fight.

BOUDICA.
Make you for the north unto the hills;
I shall unto the south distract the troops
And lead them on a chase into the woods.
I order you to go!

BLODWYNN.
                    And I refuse!

BOUDICA.
Do you forget your queen and general?

BLODWYNN.
I shall forget them sooner than my mother.

BOUDICA.
'Tis as your mother that I beg you go!

BLODWYNN.
I live or die with you – no other way.

BOUDICA.
You leave me then no choice. Lay hands on her.

The WARRIORS *seize* BLODWYNN.

I charge you take the princess, keep her safe and fly.

BLODWYNN.
No! Let go!

BOUDICA.
Ignore her pleas and threats.
Don't stop till you are far and safe. Now, go!

The sound of the ROMAN HUNTING PARTY *nears.*

BLODWYNN.
I will not go! No – Mother!

BOUDICA.
Go get you gone!
I'll find you soon, my love, I swear!

The WARRIORS *exit, taking* BLODWYNN *with them, who
shouts and screams and fights.*

Her screams and protests fade away.

The sound of the ROMAN HUNTING PARTY *is closer now.*

BOUDICA *brandishes her weapon.*

Where are you, Rome? You slouching slugabeds!
Are these your men so feeble they cannot
Outrun a woman? Come and fight me now!

BOUDICA *exits.*

Enter ROMAN SOLDIERS.

SOLDIER 1.
She came this way!

SOLDIER 2.
Where?

SOLDIER 1.
I saw her. This way. Over here – In the clearing.

SOLDIER 2.
Go!

Exit ROMAN SOLDIERS.

Their search party fades into the distance but it does not disappear – they are always close by.

BOUDICA *enters.*

BOUDICA.
I run and run, but still I cannot shake
The Romans from my scent; I feel their breath
And teeth against my neck like hunting dogs.

SOLDIER.
(*Offstage.*) She's here!

The sounds of ROMAN SOLDIERS *grows closer.*

BOUDICA *hides in the brush.*

Enter GAIUS SUETONIUS, CENTURION 2 *and* SOLDIERS.

SUETONIUS.
Where is she?

CENTURION 2.
Sir, we've scoured the trees for her, but lost all trace; the dogs have lost all scent; we cannot find neither hide nor hair.

He addresses the woods:

SUETONIUS.
Fair queen! If you can hear my voice, know this:
The battle's lost; your army's flown; the day
Is Rome's. If you do willingly submit,
You'll not be met with chains, but with respect
And be as like a guest to mighty Rome.
But if you choose to run from us and hide
You like an animal, I'll tell you now
I cannot guarantee my kindness. No?

To his men:

Look again. Form you a line, shoulder to shoulder and inch
by inch, we'll overturn this forest till we have found her.

Exit SUETONIUS *and his men.*

BOUDICA *reappears.*

BOUDICA.
Mark you how he does flatter me and thinks
That gentle tone and subtle, kindly words
Will make me girlish crawl on hand and knee
And throw myself upon his mercy? Fie!
I know what guest this man would have me for:
One bound in chains, and forced to rot away
In dungeons deep – a trophy of great Rome.
Is this how I a queen should end my days?
Andraste, please, I beg you: help me rob
This Roman lord of this the prize he seeks.
Nay, let me not be brought so low, I beg.
Goddess? I charge you: speak!
Your silence is your answer. I am lost.
What's this? Within the brush, I here can see
Some purple berries – dark as starless night.
They are the Lady Belladonna's, known
As Deadly Nightshade. 'Tis said that but one bite
Will draw the veil of night upon you, and turn
This flesh to idle clay forevermore.
Oh thank you, goddess, I knew that you would not
Abandon me to live a slave of Rome!

The sound again of ROMANS.

She is about to eat the berries – but stops.

And yet my hand is stilled – not out of fear
Of what will come of me, of that I know –
But I do fear of what will come to pass
With these my dearest daughters when I'm gone.
I'd give my crown, my title, everything
To hold them in my arms once more – To say –
Say what? What can I say?

What words could fix the fractures I have wrought?
Just as I broke my kingdom, I have torn
The intertwining vines of love that held
My girls together – I have ruined all.

A noise. BOUDICA *starts – the* ROMAN HUNTING
PARTY *is almost upon her.*

No time –

She eats the berries.

They taste them sweet – and yet they burn! They lied
To call you 'Lady Belladonna' for you are fierce!
My blood it burns, my skin, my heart, my ears –

*A noise begins to build – like the heavens themselves ripping
apart.*

Oh, listen! On the wind – I hear her now.
The wheels that turn like thunder; stamping hooves
That threat to split the world; her trumpet cry
That sure must crack the heavens. See how she flies!
The great Andraste comes for me upon
Her chariot of war, in which I'll ride
With her into the great hereafter, 'cross
The stars themselves, and like a meteor
I'll wondrous blaze across the midnight sky
And burn my name into the heavens.

The noise builds to a crescendo.

ANDRASTE *appears.*

Oh!
Sweet goddess, you are come for me! You are
More beautiful and terrifying than
I e'er could have imagined. I beg you, please:
Protect my girls as I could not; grant them
The strength and wisdom to fight the wars they will;
And each become the queen I know they are.
Would I had seen them grown...
Come take me, goddess, take me – I am done.

BOUDICA *dies.*

ANDRASTE *disappears*.

Sudden silence.

Enter SUETONIUS, CENTURION *and* SOLDIERS.

SUETONIUS *inspects the body – finds the poisonous berries on her lips and in her hand*.

SUETONIUS.
(*Aside*.) She's smaller than I thought – and yet she made
This island quake with every step she took.

CENTURION 2.
Sir?

He turns to his troops.

SUETONIUS.
Any sign of the daughter Alonna?

CENTURION 2.
No, sir.

SUETONIUS.
Bear the body hence. Bury it deep in the wood where none
shall find it. See it done with haste.

The SOLDIERS *exit bearing the body, leaving* SUETONIUS.

I must repair me now, and send report
To Rome of this our victory; and then
Prepare for what is yet to come. This fight
Was not the last: Rome will have her revenge;
So will the native clans; then us; then them;
And like a tide the war will ebb and flow
With or without me, back and forth, until
There's nothing left but sand and dust. Hail, Caesar.

Exit SUETONIUS.

Epilogue

Seven months later.

A rebel camp in the woods.

Enter ALONNA *and* BLODWYNN.

BLODWYNN.
How did you find me?

ALONNA.
It took me many months
To track you down. I thought that I had found
Your old camp near Durnovaria.

BLODWYNN.
'Twas weeks ago – we've since been on the move,
And always changing camp, so they cannot
Find where we are.

ALONNA.
And yet I found you.

BLODWYNN.
True.
But they know not this isle like you or I.

ALONNA.
They're looking for you.

BLODWYNN.
Who?

ALONNA.
The Romans.

BLODWYNN.
Are you come
To spy on me? Or have you like a dog
Been sent by Rome to come and sniff me out?
Are they approaching now? Where are they? Speak!

ALONNA.
Blodwynn, I swear, I have but talked with them –

BLODWYNN *draws her weapon.*

What are you doing?

BLODWYNN.
A spy is in my camp.

BLODWYNN *attacks* ALONNA.

ALONNA *dodges.*

BLODWYNN *attacks again.*

This time, ALONNA *draws her weapon and parries.*

Throughout the scene, they fight – and as they fight, they talk.

ALONNA.
I am your sister!

BLODWYNN.
No – my sister died
The night she slithered to the Roman camp
To sell our army out.

ALONNA.
I did not turn
A Roman traitor – I went unto their camp
To bid them lay down arms; to bid them talk
Of peace.

BLODWYNN.
Of peace?

ALONNA.
This isle has seen enough
Of bloodshed, and look where it has got us –

BLODWYNN.
Do not say 'us' for you are not our kin,
You do not know how we have fought –

ALONNA.

                              For what?
What is it that you're actually fighting for?
When all is said and done, what do you want?

BLODWYNN.

To have this isle as it once was – for those
Born and bred of it.

ALONNA.

                    And what of they
The Romans born and bred here?

BLODWYNN.

                         This land is ours,
We were the first.

ALONNA.

                 And they are now here too.
Time is a tide that we cannot turn back –
We must swim with it or we shall be drowned.

BLODWYNN.

And you would let this tide of filth come in
And drown our people? Is that what you want?

ALONNA.

I want my sister back. No more than that.
I want to sleep a single night without
The fear that when I wake the news will come
That you've been slain in battle. Blodwynn – please.
Lay down your sword and please, come home with me.
We can together sue for peace with Rome –

BLODWYNN.

You word me like a Roman! If our mother could –

ALONNA.

Our mother's dead, died fighting a war
And naught will bring her back.

BLODWYNN.

                        Do not dare speak

Of she our mother. You were not there to see
How she did die.

ALONNA.

Nor did you Blodwynn, nor
Did any one of us. She died alone.

BLODWYNN.
She died a hero.

ALONNA.

A hero and alone,
As all who choose to live them by the sword.

BLODWYNN.
You shame her honour.

ALONNA.

Death does not care for honour,
Nor land or country, tribe or language, but
He takes us all the same.

BLODWYNN.

No – when Death comes,
He will find me fighting, and so must you!

ALONNA.
I'll fight no more – for I already have
Lost friends and kinsmen, a mother to the sword,
And you would have me lose a sister too?
Blodwynn, I beg you: do not go this way,
A pathway laid in bone and trod with blood.

BLODWYNN.
I'd rather walk in blood than crawl a slave
For he your Emperor!

ALONNA.

Have it your way.

ALONNA *throws down her sword.*

BLODWYNN.
Pick up your sword. Pick it up!

ALONNA.
                                        Why?
What use is fighting, Blodwynn? Will it bring
You happiness and peaceful nights? Make this
Our home a safer place?

BLODWYNN.
                                Pick up your sword!

ALONNA.
Will fighting bring our mother back?

BLODWYNN.
                                        Shut up
And pick up your sword –

ALONNA.
                        Or what? You'll kill me? And then?
Must you kill all of Rome –

BLODWYNN.
                        Pick up –

ALONNA.
                                – all of the world,
Even yourself before you're satisfied?
Why, that way you may die just as you've dreamt –
A hero and alone, just like our mother!

BLODWYNN *screams, rushes at* ALONNA *and floors her,*
pinning her to the ground.

She raises her sword high to drive it deep into her chest…

…but instead brings it down deep into the dirt by
ALONNA*'s head.*

BLODWYNN *quickly moves away from* ALONNA, *turns*
her back to her.

ALONNA *cautiously gets to her feet and slowly approaches*
BLODWYNN, *now, shaking with anger, and reaches out.*

BLODWYNN.
No, don't touch me! I – I – I –

BLODWYNN *begins to cry.*

I miss her, Lo.

ALONNA.

> I know. I miss her too.

ALONNA *lays a hand on her sister's shoulder and* BLODWYNN *lets her.*

ALONNA *takes her in her arms and* BLODWYNN *clings to her and weeps.*

BLODWYNN.
Does it not haunt you every day? The stink
Of them; their rough and callused hands
Tearing your clothes, pinning you to the ground?
My flesh is filthy with it, my heart is soiled,
I fear that I shall ne'er be clean of it.

ALONNA.
There never shall be blood enough to wash
Our wounds full clean – we must live with the scars
And find ourselves a way to live in peace.

BLODWYNN.
I fear that I cannot – my heart still burns
With fury at what they have done to me.
I fear sometimes the fire rages so
That I will be consumed; that all this isle
Shall be engulfed; that all will burn until
There's naught but ashes left. Feel not you this?

ALONNA.
Aye, sister – that I do. But I know well
There is no use in carrying flames of hate
When they too will consume you in the end.

BLODWYNN.
Perhaps you're right.

BLODWYNN *separates herself from* ALONNA.

But fearsome as they burn,
They are the only light I now possess.

BLODWYNN *composes herself as she turns from*
ALONNA.

ALONNA.
Blodwynn –

BLODWYNN.
                    Peace, Alonna – not a word.
Do not be fooled in thinking that these tears
Have here extinguished all my anger.

ALONNA.
Sweet sister – will you not come home with me?

BLODWYNN.
Where? Amongst your Romans? That is not
Home any more. This is where I belong.
Go tell your Roman lord I shall not leave
My sword, nor shall I sleep until his kind
Are driven from my land. Go tell your lord
That this is not the end – we've just begun.

ALONNA.
Blodwynn –

BLODWYNN.
                I bid you go.

ALONNA.
                    Sister –

BLODWYNN.
                            Go!
Go get you gone before I change my mind.
And think you not to come to me again –
This is the last time that we meet as kin.

Exit BLODWYNN.

ALONNA *is left alone.*

Enter SILVIA.

SILVIA.
How did the meeting with your sister fare?

ALONNA.

> Much as I thought – or rather, as I feared.
> It's late. We should head home.

SILVIA.

> > Where's home?

ALONNA.

> > > > Indeed.
>
> I do not rightly know.

SILVIA.

> > Perhaps we'll know
> When we do find it.

ALONNA.

> > Aye – perhaps we will.
> Well, wheresoe'er it be, we should head hence.
> There's much to do, much to prepare.

SILVIA.

> > What's that?

ALONNA.

> I cannot say.

SILVIA.

> > You can't or won't?

ALONNA.

> > > I can't.
> I know what is to come – but I'm afraid
> That if I speak it loud, it will hear us.
> Can you not hear it breathing? Not feel it wait
> Like distant tempests far beyond the sky?
> Though all is seeming peace, it will not last.
> This storm will come and drown us – every one.
> Come, Silvia, let's go – we must find home
> And together build us levies to hold it back,
> The thunder soon will come, and this land will crack.

Exeunt.

End.

Helen Edmundson
ANNA KARENINA *after* Tolstoy
THE CLEARING
CORAM BOY *after* Gavin
GONE TO EARTH *after* Webb
THE HERESY OF LOVE
LIFE IS A DREAM *after* Calderón
MARY SHELLEY
THE MILL ON THE FLOSS *after* Eliot
MOTHER TERESA IS DEAD
QUEEN ANNE
SWALLOWS AND AMAZONS *after* Ransome
WAR AND PEACE *after* Tolstoy

Liz Lochhead
BLOOD AND ICE
DRACULA *after* Stoker
EDUCATING AGNES ('The School for Wives') *after* Molière
GOOD THINGS
LIZ LOCHHEAD: FIVE PLAYS
MARY QUEEN OF SCOTS GOT
HER HEAD CHOPPED OFF
MEDEA *after* Euripides
MISERYGUTS ('The Miser') & TARTUFFE *after* Molière
PERFECT DAYS
THEBANS *after* Euripides & Sophocles
THON MAN MOLIÈRE

Conor McPherson
DUBLIN CAROL
GIRL FROM THE NORTH COUNTRY *with* Bob Dylan
McPHERSON PLAYS: ONE
McPHERSON PLAYS: TWO
McPHERSON PLAYS: THREE
THE NEST *after* Franz Xaver Kroetz
THE NIGHT ALIVE
PORT AUTHORITY
THE SEAFARER
SHINING CITY
THE VEIL
THE WEIR

Rona Munro
THE ASTRONAUT'S CHAIR
THE HOUSE OF BERNARDA ALBA *after* Lorca
THE INDIAN BOY
IRON
THE JAMES PLAYS
THE LAST WITCH
LITTLE EAGLES
LONG TIME DEAD
THE MAIDEN STONE
MARY BARTON *after* Gaskell
PANDAS
SCUTTLERS
STRAWBERRIES IN JANUARY *from* de la Chenelière
YOUR TURN TO CLEAN THE STAIR & FUGUE

Mark Rylance
I AM SHAKESPEARE
NICE FISH

Jessica Swale
BLUE STOCKINGS
NELL GWYNN

Phoebe Waller-Bridge
FLEABAG